PETER LITTLEJOHNS
DAVID J. HUNTER
ALBERT WEALE
JACQUELINE JOHNSON
TOSLIMA KHATUN

MAKING
HEALTH PUBLIC

A Manifesto for a New Social Contract

POLICY PRESS **SHORTS** RESEARCH

First published in Great Britain in 2024 by

Policy Press, an imprint of
Bristol University Press
University of Bristol
1-9 Old Park Hill
Bristol
BS2 8BB
UK
t: +44 (0)117 374 6645
e: bup-info@bristol.ac.uk

Details of international sales and distribution partners are available at
policy.bristoluniversitypress.co.uk

© Bristol University Press 2024

British Library Cataloguing in Publication Data
A catalogue record for this book is available from the British Library

ISBN 978-1-4473-7126-7 hardcover
ISBN 978-1-4473-7127-4 ePub
ISBN 978-1-4473-7128-1 ePdf

The right of Peter Littlejohns, David J. Hunter, Albert Weale, Jacqueline Johnson and
Toslima Khatun to be identified as authors of this work has been asserted by them in
accordance with the Copyright, Designs and Patents Act 1988.

Cover design: Bristol University Press
Front cover image: iStock/CasarsaGuru
Bristol University Press and Policy Press use environmentally responsible
print partners.
Printed and bound in Great Britain by CPI Group (UK) Ltd,
Croydon, CR0 4YY

FSC
www.fsc.org
MIX
Paper | Supporting
responsible forestry
FSC® C013604

Contents

List of figures

List of abbreviations

ADPH	Association of Directors of Public Health
ART	antiretroviral therapy
CMO	Chief Medical Officer
COPD	chronic obstructive pulmonary disease
COSLA	Convention of Scottish Local Authorities
DH	Department of Health
DHSC	Department of Health and Social Care
HiAP	Health in All Policies
ICS	integrated care system
NAO	National Audit Office
NERVTAG	New and Emerging Respiratory Virus Threats Advisory Group
NHS	National Health Service
NHSE	National Health Service England
NICE	National Institute for Health and Care Excellence
OBR	Office for Budget Responsibility
OHID	Office for Health Improvement and Disparities
PAC	Public Accounts Committee
PHE	Public Health England
PHS	Public Health Scotland
PHW	Public Health Wales
PrEP	pre-exposure prophylaxis
SAGE	Scientific Advisory Group for Emergencies
UKHSA	United Kingdom Health Security Agency
WHO	World Health Organisation

Preface

There is now general agreement that the UK is facing a public health crisis. Improvements in life expectancy have stalled, health inequalities are continuing to widen, obesity and alcohol misuse are placing an increasing strain on health services, and urban air pollution is now widely recognised as a serious health hazard. However, consensus on possible solutions is absent. COVID-19 revealed the weaknesses of the UK's public health system – once thought to be among the best in the world. While we are still waiting for the official Covid-19 Inquiry to report its findings, an increasing number of studies are demonstrating where the problems lie – not only in infectious disease control but more generally in public health. Our own research study took place in 2021 and 2022, and sought to understand the circumstances surrounding the abolition of the main institution responsible for public health in England – Public Health England – and its replacement by the UK Health Security Agency and the Office for Health Improvement and Disparities. The publications that emerged from that original study are detailed in an appendix.

Our findings convinced us that what is urgently needed is much broader than simply targeted interventions. A fundamental public policy debate is necessary to stimulate interest in the vital importance of public health and a new approach initiated. We have come to the conclusion that a completely new way of thinking about public health is required, and that would only be achieved by establishing by a new social contract for the UK population. We are not alone in thinking that fundamental change is required. The Institute for Public Policy Research (IPPR, 2023) recently published its first interim report on health in the UK, advocating a new Health and Prosperity Act supported by a Committee on Health and Prosperity – modelled on the Climate Change Committee and designed to independently advise on the above mission (and hold all governments accountable to it).

Our book does not try to revisit all the theories and initiatives to improve public health but explores some of the fundamental barriers and why interventions (even those based on good evidence) are not adequately implemented. We address several key political and governance issues around the social contract idea. We build on the thinking outlined in the history of public health by David Hunter et al, *The Public Health System in England* (Policy Press, 2010). We highlight a number of key concerns: the failings of short-term versus long-term political commitment and strategy when dealing with complex problems; that many of the key public health problems cluster around the same deprived social groups, so tackling health inequalities is key to any interventions; the lack of cross-government working and the need to stop silo-driven departmentalism, since all public health issues transcend any single department or policy sector; tackling the commercial determinants of health, which is becoming harder thanks to Brexit and the absence of health concerns in new trade deals; and finally, we address the central-local issues as power is devolved from Westminster.

The list is long and daunting, but unless we privilege these more deep-seated and generic issues (rather than creating individual policies and lists of interventions around obesity, alcohol misuse, mental health, pollution, water quality) we will get more of the same.

We believe now is the time to be bold. With the UK Covid-19 Inquiry ongoing and a general election in the offing, this debate should be accessible for all to participate in.

PL, DJH, AW, JJ and TK,
22 September 2023

Note on Figure 2.1

We wish to acknowledge that the text of Figure 2.1 is smaller than the images we would normally publish. The decision to include this image was made because it is integral to the book's content. A PDF of the image in its original form can be viewed at: https://policy.bristoluniversitypress.co.uk/making-health-public

ONE

The challenges of public health

The crisis of public health

The UK faces a health crisis. In 2018–20 growth in life expectancy stalled for women and declined for men, taking men back to the level in 2012–14 (ONS, 2021). Although the immediate cause was the outbreak of COVID-19 in 2020, a slowing-down in improvements in life expectancy had been happening for a decade, particularly affecting the most deprived 10 per cent of the population, and falling or stagnating for some groups (Marmot, 2022). In other comparable economies, life expectancy has increased at a faster rate (OECD, 2023), so the latest figures are the culmination of a longer term trend. But COVID-19 also led to a surge in the number of those of the working-age population being unfit for work through extended sickness. Before 2020, less than 5 per cent of the relevant population were unfit for work in this way; by 2022, it was more than 6 per cent (Neville and Borrett, 2023). COVID-19 hit the UK population hard because there had been a failure of public health planning over many years. The result was the growth in a number of health risks that bring illness in their wake and impose severe strains on the National Health Service (NHS). The omens in respect of these health risks look poor.

Consider obesity. As Figure 1.1 shows, obesity rates are high in the UK when set against comparable western European countries. While obesity has increased in all the high-income countries, rates in the UK more than tripled between 1975 and 2016, whereas France and Germany showed much lower rates of growth, as did other European countries like Italy. To be sure, the UK does not equal the US or Australia in its obesity, but it is closer to them than to its European neighbours. Obesity is an important public health measure because being obese leads to a predictor of poor health, causing strain on the skeleton and increasing the risk of fatal heart attacks or stroke. It also leads to an increased risk of type 2 diabetes, a disease that is responsible for some 10 per cent of NHS expenditure.

Consider alcohol misuse. As Figure 1.2 shows, the disease burden implied by alcohol and drug misuse tripled in the UK between 1990 and 2015. While there has been a reduction in the trend since 2015, the UK again stands out by comparison with its European neighbours, to which it was very close in 1990. Ill health arising from alcohol misuse can develop over the long term and is a major contributor to depression and other mental illnesses. Moreover, the disease burden of alcohol misuse is only one part of the public health story. Many town and city centres in the UK are in effect no-go areas on Friday and Saturday nights. Alcohol is no normal commodity.

Consider air pollution. Urban air pollution is increasingly coming to be recognised as a major health hazard. A report from the Royal College of Physicians (2016) explained the physiological effects of indoor and outdoor air pollution and implicated air pollution in a range of diseases, including cerebrovascular disease, chronic obstructive pulmonary disease (COPD), ischaemic heart disease, lower respiratory infections, and trachea, bronchus and lung cancers, all leading to increased deaths and ill health. In December 2020 Southwark Coroner's Court in London found that air pollution had 'made a material contribution' to the death of a nine-year-old child (Marshall, 2020). The Chief Medical Officer's annual report

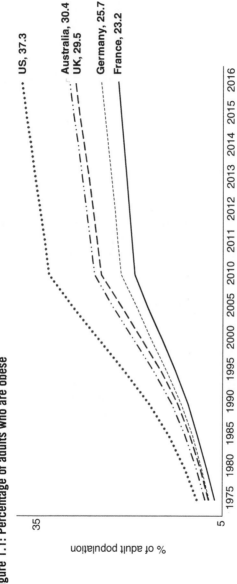

Figure 1.1: Percentage of adults who are obese

Source: Own calculation from Our World in Data. https://ourworldindata.org/grapher/share-of-adults-defined-as-obese?tab=chart&country=

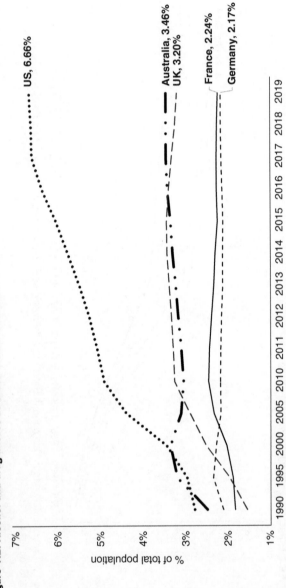

Figure 1.2: Alcohol and drug misuse as share of disease burden

Source: Own calculation from Our World in Data. https://ourworldindata.org/grapher/alcohol-drug-use-disorders-share-total-dise ase?tab=chart

of 2022 (Chief Medical Officer's Report, 2022) focused on air pollution, suggesting that the mortality burden of air pollution in England was between 26,000 and 38,000 deaths a year, alongside the avoidable chronic ill health effects.

Consider health inequalities. Lack of public health measures do not strike the population randomly. Instead, they all too often sharpen existing health inequalities. The UK problem with health inequalities has been noted by commentators such as the King's Fund (Murray, 2021). Although concern over health inequalities and how they can best be tackled has been at the heart of much public health policy and practice over many decades, success in reducing those inequalities has been limited. Indeed, since 2010 and the arrival of the coalition government, with its twin ideological foci (on austerity in order to get public spending in order, and on shrinking the state to reduce the size of government), social and regional health inequalities have widened significantly. Cuts to local government spending have been a particular driver of these developments (Lewer and Bibby, 2021; Marshall et al, 2021; Murphie, 2023). With another round of austerity announced towards the end of 2022 to tackle inflation and government debt, combined with a cost of living crisis, the position can only deteriorate further in the coming years.

The pandemic in 2020 shone a spotlight on all these long-standing – and worsening – social and economic weaknesses. A review of the data undertaken by Public Health England (PHE) confirmed that the impact of COVID-19 'has replicated existing health inequalities and, in some cases, has increased them' (Public Health England, 2020: 4). Although the largest disparity found was by age, with people aged over 80 seventy times more likely to die than those under 40, the risk of dying was also higher in males than females, in those living in more deprived areas, and was higher in Black, Asian and minority ethnic (BAME) groups.

The World Health Organization's (WHO) health equity status report calculated that 90 per cent of health inequalities can be explained by financial insecurity, poor quality housing, social exclusion, and lack of decent work and poor working conditions (WHO, 2019). While access to healthcare is important, it only accounts for 10 per cent of differences in health status across different socioeconomic groups.

Shortly before the first national lockdown in mid-March 2020, a damning report appeared, from Michael Marmot and his team, which revisited his strategic review of health inequalities in England conducted in 2010 (Marmot et al, 2020). The stark conclusion reached was that the UK's population is in a much poorer state of health than a decade ago and social inequalities are wider. In terms of overall health, since 2010 the rate of increase in life expectancy had slowed and, by 2018, had more or less ground to a halt. Only the US and Iceland fared worse. When it came to health inequalities, these continued to increase, with the more deprived places experiencing a higher mortality rate and shorter life expectancy. Whereas during the 2000s the gap in life expectancy between the poorest areas and the rest had narrowed, over the decade from 2010 it increased.

When COVID-19 finally struck the UK, after the government had originally played down its likely impact, Marmot noted that 'the same set of influences that led England and the UK looking unhealthy in the decade after 2010 led us to having the worst excess mortality figures in Europe' (Marmot, 2020). In their evidence to the COVID-19 Inquiry, Bambra and Marmot conclude: 'the health picture, then, coming into the pandemic was stalling life expectancy, increased regional and deprivation-based health inequalities, and worsening health for the poorest in society' (Bambra and Marmot, 2023: paragraph 46, p 23).

Given the deterioration in health and rise in inequalities, it is little wonder that COVID-19 has highlighted the importance of obesity as a risk factor and raised concerns over alcohol and dietary habits and mental health. These behaviours tend to cluster among those social groups living in deprived places. They are also more marked in the north as another report on the North–South divide concludes (Bambra et al, 2020). Mortality rates during the first wave of the virus (March to July 2020) were higher in the Northern Powerhouse areas than the rest of England, and economic outcomes, particularly unemployment rates, were hardest hit in these areas.

The problems of obesity, alcohol misuse, air pollution and heath inequalities are only a small selection of the urgent problems of public health. Climate change will lead to an increase in extreme weather events, whether they be heatwaves or cold snaps (Lancet Countdown, 2022). Antimicrobial resistance poses a global threat to health. Dispersed chemicals in the environment pose a range of threats. And, most obviously, COVID-19 reminds us that the dangers of infectious diseases have not gone away, something that should have been apparent before the pandemic with rising rates of tuberculosis, or the threats of visitors to the UK introducing diseases like Ebola.

Against the background of these extensive public health hazards, there is a major puzzle for the analysis of public policy. Studies routinely show good returns on investments in public health measures. For example, in a review of studies from a number of countries, Masters et al (2017) show that a wide variety of public health measures produce a good return on investment over time. These measures range from smoking cessation programmes, community-based falls prevention programmes, cycle and pedestrian trails, speed controls on vehicles on roads, to vaccination and folic fortification of bread. Conversely, a failure to address long-standing risk factors for health can create costs for a medical system, as is the case with diabetes.

The insight is not new. The value of investing in public health has been stressed by knowledgeable commentators over decades. As far back as the 1970s, the UK was discussing 'Prevention and Health' (Department of Health and Social Security, 1976) and Canada's Lalonde (1974) report (Clark, 2020). The arguments were that medical services would find it increasingly hard to cope with increased demand on their resources unless there was a significant investment in upstream measures to reduce that demand. Most recently, the same arguments have been revisited by the Hewitt Review into the new integrated care systems (ICSs) introduced into the NHS in England. The review argues that 'unless we transform our model of health and care, as a nation we will not achieve the health and wellbeing we want for all our communities' (Hewitt, 2023: 4). As Hewitt rightly points out, 'we should never mistake NHS policy for health policy' (ibid). She goes on to argue that shifting the focus towards public health measures will require a decisive shift in resources and recommends that the share of total NHS budgets at ICS level going towards prevention should be increased by at least 1 per cent over the next five years. The review also argues that the public health grant to local authorities needs to be increased after eight years of a real-terms squeeze on their funding. Picking up on a theme which is gaining ground in health policy circles, Hewitt argues that instead of viewing health and care as a cost, we need to align all partners around the creation of health value.

In making these proposals, Hewitt confronts head-on the claim that the much-needed focus on prevention and population health cannot occur until the immediate pressures on the NHS post-pandemic (for example, the elective care backlog) are addressed. In reply, she argues that this is a false argument, and that there is never a perfect time to make the necessary shift in priorities. 'This is what has always happened before, and must not happen this time' (Hewitt, 2023: paragraph 1.12, p 12).

Moreover, there are no problems in identifying what might be priority policy areas. The Faculty of Public Health has produced a number of policy briefs with specific ideas as to what would be needed (Faculty of Public Health, 2023). Recommendations include a government commitment to more green spaces for their health-enhancing effects, more stringent control of water pollution, funding for work on antibiotic resistance, commitment to immunisation programmes, a food policy that promoted healthier foods, a harm-reduction approach to drug use, controls on pricing and marketing of alcohol, and support for government programmes to keep energy costs in check. The question is not one of feasibility, but of a willingness to engage with the issues and make the requisite policy and political choices.

But if, as Hewitt said, the neglect of public health measures is something that has always happened before, that is evidence that there are structural and other barriers to change that need to be tackled if the neglect is not to happen again. If public health investments are good value for money and knowledgeable observers have stressed repeatedly that, while invaluable, the NHS is not a health service but an illness service, why have we not seen more government action? What prevents effective prevention rather than a moralising focus on lifestyles? To understand the answer to that question, we need to identify what public health measures involve, and why governments, particularly UK governments, have found it hard to implement those measures.

The challenges of public health

Public health has been defined as the 'science and art of preventing disease, prolonging life and promoting, protecting and improving health through the organised efforts of society' (Acheson, 1988). This was the definition adopted by the Acheson review into public health in England in 1988. Building on this definition and expanding its elements, the Faculty of Public Health has endorsed the concept of the three domains of public health (Griffiths et al, 2005). They are: health improvement; health protection; and health service quality improvement.

> The *health improvement* domain covers key aspects of activity to reduce inequalities, working with partners not only in the NHS but in other sectors such as education

and workplaces. It involves engagement with structural determinants such as housing and employment, as well as working with individuals and their families within communities to improve health and prevent disease through adopting healthier life-styles.

Health protection includes the prevention and control of infectious diseases as well as response to emergencies, be they the result of a chemical or radiation disaster or of bioterrorism. It engages with the regulation for clean air, water and food as well as preventing or dealing with environmental health hazards.

Health service quality improvement includes engagement in service delivery, promoting clinically effective practice particularly through promoting evidence-based care, supporting clinical governance, planning and prioritising services, and engaging in appropriate research, audit and evaluation.

The three domains are not, of course, unrelated areas of activity. Sometimes they overlap and are interdependent. This was well illustrated during the COVID-19 pandemic, when it became clear that obesity was a significant risk factor in contracting the disease and in experiencing its progression to more serious forms, so that concerns of health protection and health promotion were joined. Both were linked to the need to improve the quality of care. So the three domains can be used to describe the services to be delivered, the core skills, knowledge and competencies that are needed, and the roles and responsibilities of those delivering them.

Yet although often interrelated in practice, the three domains can be analytically distinguished and are sometimes found separately. In the rest of this work we shall focus on health protection and health improvement, which are the core activities of the public health system outside the NHS, and which have distinct issue characteristics that affect policy making and implementation. In particular, these characteristics are related to the wide-ranging agenda of public health, the focus on prevention, the need for precaution, the social rootedness of health inequalities, the need for interorganisational policy making and political leadership, each of which provides its own distinctive challenge.

These various challenges have their origin in the fact that health and illness are in large measure socially determined. The phrase 'the social determinants of health and illness' is liable to misinterpretation. To some, the term might suggest that individuals and policy makers are trapped in a system that controls them and that they cannot control. But that is not what is meant by the concept of social determinants.

To see what it does mean, it is useful to highlight the implicit contrast between the social determinants of health on the one hand, and other determinants on the other. Thus, those who point to the social determinants of health often have in mind a contrast with the medical determinants of health. When the NHS was founded, it was assumed that the elimination of financial barriers to medical care would bring about a more equal distribution of health in the population. In fact, health inequalities have tended to increase since the establishment of the NHS. The reason is that medical care can only make a relatively small contribution to the overall health of the population. Unless social and economic conditions are tackled, medical care free at point of use can continue to exist alongside continuing health inequalities.

The second contrast to highlight the meaning of the idea of the social determinants of health is that between social factors and physiological or genetic factors. Thus, genetic factors cannot be responsible for the increase in obesity during the last fifty years, since genetic change is too slow compared to social change to account for the swiftness of that rise. Instead we have to look to increasing levels of disposable income, changing transport patterns such that people walk less, and a food industry that finds it profitable to sell high-energy but low-nutrition foods.

The role of the food industry is one portion of what has been termed the commercial determinants of health (Friel et al, 2023; Gilmore et al, 2023; Kickbusch et al, 2023; Lacy-Nichols et al, 2023). The commercial determinants of health may incline towards increasing ill health as with high-energy/low-nutrition foods. However, commercial incentives may also incline toward promoting health. Makers of sports equipment have an interest in encouraging people to be healthier through more exercise. The increase in low-alcohol drinks in recent years has in part been a consequence of a reduction in the demand for alcohol among younger age groups, and in part a response to tighter regulation. And increased demand for active travel benefits suppliers of cycles and those re-engineering roads and highways.

So when we speak about the social determinants of health, we are referring to the fact that health and ill health have their origins in complex social and economic conditions: conditions that can encourage or discourage healthy lifestyles, or conditions, like environmental pollution, that can be hazardous in themselves. It is this rootedness in complex social and economic conditions that makes for the challenges of public health policy. If vigorous public health measures are to be pursued, those challenges will need to be overcome.

The challenge of a wide-ranging agenda

The wide range of risks to health with which public health is concerned implies a wide-ranging agenda of policy issues, be they regulation to control environmental hazards, the composition of foods, the sale of dangerous substances, vaccination, pricing, contingency planning, or the provision of accessible information and advice. Moreover, given that ill health and, in particular, inequalities in ill health are rooted in social conditions (for example, poor housing or lack of access to exercise spaces), the policy mandate of any public health system is wide and varied. Given this wide mandate, those bodies responsible for public health will have to make a decision as to how to balance the different elements and how to set the agenda of policy priority.

Some public health issues, most notably outbreaks of serious epidemics, can rise suddenly to the top of the agenda through the logic of focusing events (Birkland, 1998), a change in the state of the world that potentially highlights the shortcomings of routine policy. Other public health issues, however, display a logic of steady cumulative growth in seriousness and, therefore, of policy attention span. Air pollution and obesity, for example, have had adverse health effects over decades, but there is no one point where the graph of those effects shows a clear point of inflection. In consequence they are typically less visible on the policy agenda. In the case of air pollution, for example, problems have persisted for some time but policy attention has only turned to the question in recent years.

The wide range of possible health hazards and the varied measures that might be required to address them therefore confront policy makers with the challenge of determining priorities, simultaneously requiring a wide attention span, so that steadily accumulating hazards are attended to as well as emergencies. The skill needed to analyse the problems and devise suitable policies is correspondingly wide, involving, for example, laboratory sciences, epidemiology, physiology, psychology and behavioural studies, economics and spatial planning to name but a few. The problem of priorities is likely to be particularly important when seeking to persuade high-level policy makers and finance ministries of the need to plan and make provision for possible but not certain contingencies so that latent as well as manifest problems are addressed.

The challenge of prevention

Public health is concerned with the prevention of ill health. Preventive interventions are conventionally divided into three categories:

- Primary prevention aims to prevent disease or injury before it occurs. It consists in preventing exposure to health risks (for example, hazardous substances in the environment or workplace), as well as education in healthy living and vaccination against communicable diseases.
- Secondary prevention aims to reduce the impact of a disease or injury that has already occurred; for example, through screening programmes or modification of work tasks.
- Tertiary prevention aims to reduce the effects of already existing illnesses or injuries; for example, through stroke rehabilitation programmes or therapies to manage episodes of depression.

Interventions at the primary end are 'upstream' attempts to formulate policies with the aim of reducing the onset of disease; for example, reductions in obesity or poor diet that will reduce the onset of type 2 diabetes. This is not to say that there is a sharp distinction between public health and medical intervention, as the example of vaccination illustrates. However, what does mark out public health interventions is that as well as the medical sciences, public health measures necessarily employ non-medical policy instruments such as environmental regulation, urban planning measures or safety regulation of food and drink.

The bias against prevention has a number of causes. Firstly, there are the immediate pressures that come from public dissatisfaction with the state of the NHS, most obviously problems of waiting times, access to accident and emergency services and the availability of GPs for appointments, so that the temptation to spend money on the urgent is politically hard to resist. Secondly, spending money on medical services is tangible, in a way that spending money on prevention is not, since effective preventive policies reduce adverse events that otherwise would have occurred, but when they are successful, no one sees the counterfactual of the disease that would have occurred had those policies not been adopted. Thirdly, prevention involves being able to act across a number of distinct domains of public policy – for example, transport, food, environmental and spatial planning policies – but in the absence of strong and committed leadership, the interorganisational cooperation required is intrinsically difficult (see below).

The challenge of precaution

Prevention and precaution overlap, but they are not coextensive. Prevention may be necessary even when there is a clear and present danger to health, such as the discovery of contaminated foodstuffs leading to their withdrawal from sale. But the key idea behind a precautionary approach is to adopt policies that prevent or mitigate the risks of injury or disease even when there is a low probability that an adverse event will occur. Moreover, since not all risks to health can be prevented (for example, weather events that pose a risk to health such as a heatwave or severe cold), precaution requires contingency planning for such health risks. Precaution is required for an incident that may or may not happen, or, if the incident is unavoidable, having countermeasures in place.

A precautionary approach to policy presents its own distinctive challenges, in particular how to make policy in the face of uncertainty, particularly in relation to low probability events. Not only is this difficult in itself, it presents officials – particularly elected officials – with the need to determine priorities among a range of unknowns, since of all the adverse events that could occur only a relatively small number will occur. In circumstances in which public spending is tightly constrained, a failure of precaution is all too likely, since precautionary action will involve spending resources on something that might not happen, taking those same resources away from a problem that definitely exists. A failure of precaution in this sense was illustrated by the lack of stocked personal protective equipment (PPE) equipment during the COVID-19 pandemic.

The challenge here is, in part, one of time horizons. Dealing with urgent problems too easily distracts policy attention – itself a scare resource – away from important problems. But a failure to pay attention to important public health problems makes it more likely that they will become urgent in the future. In this way, the bias against prevention also becomes a bias against precaution. Given that the beneficiaries of public health measures are future unknown statistical lives, there is likely to be a policy and political bias towards known present lives in danger. However, at some point in the future, those unknown statistical lives will turn into present known lives. A failure of precaution will show up eventually.

The challenge of interorganisational collaboration

The governance of public health involves a number of different organisations, and the responsibility for public health is distributed around different organisations. Although a body like PHE or its successor the UK Health Security Agency (UKHSA) may have designated responsibility for public health, such central government bodies have to interact both with the corresponding bodies in the devolved home nations and with local government. The importance of this intergovernmental working was highlighted during the COVID-19 pandemic, when the failure of the Test and Trace regime was in part due to a failure to involve local government sufficiently. It is well known that interorganisational collaboration, both in the public and the private sectors, is generally difficult, requiring different bodies with their own priorities and perspectives to move beyond silo thinking.

Public health poses additional problems of interorganisational collaboration, however. Given the origins of ill health in a broad range of social and economic circumstances, the scope of public health policy necessarily intersects with the policy responsibilities of government departments other than those with a specific health remit. This intersectoral role for a public health agency has been widely noted and commented on in connection with governments all around the world and is the underlying reason for the perspective of 'health in all policies'.

By way of illustration, the National Audit Office (NAO) has usefully identified some twelve central departments of state, other than the Department of Health and Social Care, whose policy responsibilities could affect people's health. They include: Levelling Up, Housing and Communities; HM Revenue and Customs; Work and Pensions; Justice; Business, Energy and Industrial Strategy; Environment, Food and Rural Affairs; Digital, Culture, Media and Sport; Education; Transport; the Treasury; and the Home Office (NAO, 2022: 71). Figure 1.3 reproduces the NAO figure, which maps these various ministries in relation to the specific health issues whose policies they may affect.

Moreover, as the NAO itself acknowledges, this list is just a sample of the departments of state whose work affects health. For example, if we focus on the case of air pollution, dealing with that hazard at source potentially involves more departments than Environment, Food and Rural Affairs. Vehicle emission standards are internationally agreed, and so international trade is affected as well as relations with international bodies like the European Union or the World Trade Organization. If taxes are used as instruments of pollution control, both the Treasury and HM Revenue and Customs are involved. Town planning and the design of private and public transport systems are relevant, so that both Transport and Housing are involved. If the urban area includes a port, then the public authorities responsible for the regulation of shipping will also be involved.

The involvement of different actors makes for conflicting policy priorities, particularly when some departments of state, most notably the Treasury in the UK, are more powerful than other departments. Different departments will have their own remits and policy commitments, and their concerns may not be consistent with those of a public health body. As a result, policy conflicts may replace policy coordination. Making cities accessible

Figure 1.3: Departmental responsibilities for factors influencing health outcomes

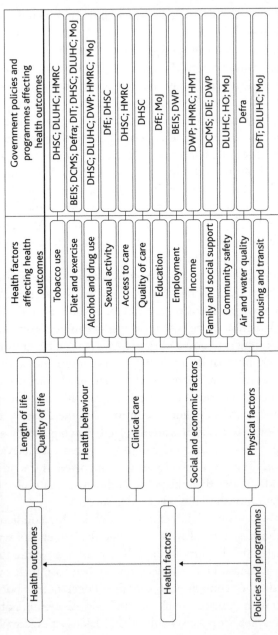

Source: Adapted from National Audit Office, *Integrated Care Systems: Joining Up Local Services to Improve Health Outcomes* (London: National Audit Office, 2022), p. 71, Figure 21. https://www.nao.org.uk/wp-content/uploads/2022/10/Integrated-Care-Systems-Fundingand-accountability-for-local-health-and-care.pdf.

to the private car, which over a number of years has been the goal of transport ministries and town planners, may increase the pollution that is at the root of various diseases. Competition policy may support the supply of cheaper alcohol. International tourism makes easier the communication of disease. The policy priorities of non-health departments may be perfectly legitimate in themselves, but create increased health problems as the unintended by-product of social and economic activities. Public health issues prompt questions not only of interdepartmental coordination – questions that are difficult enough in themselves – but also question how conflicting priorities that are hardwired into departmental standard operating procedures are reconciled and resolved by government as a whole.

The challenge of political leadership

One senior medical adviser is reported to have said on pandemic preparation that it involves 'telling government what they don't want to know, to spend money they don't have, on something they don't think will happen' (cited in Ricketts, 2021: 114). The challenge of political leadership is to rise above the routine pressures of the policy process to ensure the pursuit of the important and not just the urgent. For those with specific policy responsibilities, this means being able to spell out clearly what are the crucial priorities of public health planning and being robust in securing the resources for those priorities. For heads of government, it means ensuring that interdepartmental and intergovernmental collaboration is not frustrated by turf wars in which departments are eager to guard their own interests at the expense of a more general interest. It means being honest with the public about the trade-offs that policy choices involve, abandoning the rhetoric of the UK having 'world-beating' systems that has become so prevalent in recent years. In short, the art of political leadership is to assert the public health interest as a priority of government action that overrides business as usual.

The old and new social contracts

The barriers to effective public health policy that we have discussed so far reflect the characteristics of public health as an issue. Health prevention and health promotion address a large number of varied issues and call on a wide range of instruments. The public health system is organisationally complex and involves interorganisational collaboration, something that is always hard. Interorganisational collaboration requires responsibility to be shared among a number of different governmental bodies, not all of whom will take the advancement of health as their primary goal. And only clear political leadership will ensure the implementation of the relevant measures.

However, beyond these process barriers there lies, in our view, a deeper problem of public philosophy. Governments will not act on difficult problems unless they believe that it is vital that they do so and see the urgency of doing so. Ultimately, then, the problem of public health requires a change in the dominant public philosophy that has guided so much of public policy for the last 40 years. Effective public health policy requires a new social contract.

The old social contract, which became firmly entrenched in the UK in the 1980s, described itself as an individualist one. It made consumer choice the litmus test of public policy and was sceptical of state-led solutions to social problems. If people choose to use their private cars rather than take public transport, then public policy should accommodate and facilitate that preference. If they choose to eat junk food and drink too much, then public policy should not intervene. If they ignore health warnings, then that is their lookout. If they prefer not to be vaccinated against a highly transmissible disease, that is up to them.

This individualist philosophy is in some respects a noble one. There is something important in drawing attention to the value of personal responsibility in social life. There is also much that is valuable in living in a tolerant society that will inevitably allow people to go to hell in their own way. The problem with the stress on personal choice and liberty is not that it gives importance to individual fulfilment and choice. It is that in doing so, it is incomplete. It ignores the spillover effects that make the individual choices of some a burden for others. If individuals choose to drive their cars to work, they make the streets less tolerable for pedestrians, particularly children, for whom the walk to school or work may be an essential element in their daily exercise. If individuals choose to eat junk food and drink too much, they will inevitably place extra demand on the health services for which all pay, all too often placing pressing demand on accident and emergency services on Friday and Saturday nights. If individuals ignore health warnings, then their heart attacks, strokes and cancers will have to be treated. If they refuse to be vaccinated, they become a walking health hazard for others.

In addition to ignoring spillover effects, the old individualist social contract was also incomplete in another way. In making individual consumer choice the guiding principle of public policy, it ignored the production of those goods that can only be provided as public or collective goods. While those with the money may buy adequate medical care, they cannot buy protection from infectious diseases, the monitoring of the health status of the population, the preparedness of public and social services in case of emergencies, like flooding or a heat wave, or the environmental regulation that protects against water, soil and air pollution. Nor can the old individualism provide the infrastructure of scientific research and the public dissemination of knowledge on which sound health policy must rest. It is only a seeming paradox to say that individualism of the sort that leads to general human fulfilment and security requires collective organisation at its foundation. The old individualism was, therefore, what we might call a vulgar individualism, defined by the doctrine that says that that government is best that governs least. Yet, without the public goods that only governments can secure, life is – as the seventeenth-century political philosopher Thomas Hobbes stressed – 'solitary, poor, nasty, brutish, and short'.

The new social contract that we advocate in this book moves beyond a vulgar individualism to what we shall call a social individualism that prioritises the supply of those public goods that individuals cannot provide for themselves, and which are the conditions for individual choice and fulfilment. But the construction of a new social contract must start with where we are, not with where we hope to get to. To improve policy, we need to understand the conditions under which it is made, and the choices that have taken us to the point where we now stand. So our first task is to understand how we have come to be in our present state of crisis and what the possibilities are for a programme of vigorous public health measures. Chapter 2 provides a history of public health administration and policy in England, culminating in a discussion of the highly contestable decision to abolish PHE in the middle of the COVID-19 pandemic and replace it with two new bodies whose processes and remits needed to be worked out in the middle of the crisis. Chapter 3 discusses the organisation and administration of public health agencies in the home nations, as a way of showing how the task of public health is less about the precise configuration of organisations and more about the possibilities of learning from varieties of approaches. Chapter 4 looks at the principles and processes of the two bodies that replaced PHE and what opportunities the new organisation of the NHS in England offers for public health. Chapter 5 outlines the case for a new social contract and concludes with a public health manifesto that a new social contract would require. As we work our way from the nuts and bolts of organisational design, through the principles of public health interventions, we shall eventually find ourselves laying out the elements of the new social contract that is required to make health public.

TWO

Public health in England, 2013 to 2020

Chapter 1 laid out the challenges of public health together with the intrinsic dilemmas and conflicts involved in making health truly public. The source of those dilemmas is to be found in the fact that public health identifies many sources of ill health in the determinants that are formed in complex social and economic systems. Ill health is the effect of multiple causes. In terms of governmental organisation, this means that a public health body must interact with a wide range of agencies and sectors across government. However, it also means that any such interaction needs to be based on a strong and well-resourced core of public health bodies, at different levels of government, which can identify health problems and formulate effective policies, even when those policies need the cooperation of other departments of state.

In this chapter we look at the history of those core organisations in England between 2013 when Public Health England (PHE) was established by the 2012 Health and Social Care Act, and 2020 when the announcement was made that it was to be abolished. Our aim is to show how the dilemmas and challenges identified in the previous chapter played out during this period. Figure 2.1 summarises the key points in the timeline.

Figure 2.1: Timeline for English public health developments

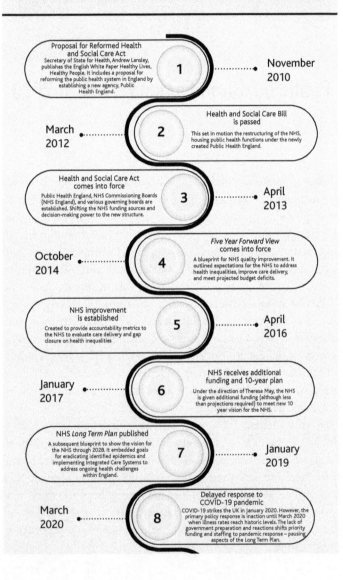

UK public health policy: a decade in review

Proposal for Reformed Health and Social Care Act
Secretary of State for Health, Andrew Lansley, publishes the English White Paper Healthy Lives, Healthy People. It includes a proposal for reforming the public health system in England by establishing a new agency, Public Health England.

1 — November 2010

Health and Social Care Bill is passed
This set in motion the restructuring of the NHS, housing public health functions under the newly created Public Health England.

March 2012 — 2

Health and Social Care Act comes into force
Public Health England, NHS Commissioning Boards (NHS England), and various governing boards are established. Shifting the NHS funding sources and decision-making power to the new structure.

3 — April 2013

Five Year Forward View comes into force
A blueprint for NHS quality improvement. It outlined expectations for the NHS to address health inequalities, improve care delivery, and meet projected budget deficits.

October 2014 — 4

NHS improvement is established
Created to provide accountability metrics to the NHS to evaluate care delivery and gap closure on health inequalities

5 — April 2016

NHS receives additional funding and 10-year plan
Under the direction of Theresa May, the NHS is given additional funding (although less than projections required) to meet new 10 year vision for the NHS.

January 2017 — 6

NHS Long Term Plan published
A subsequent blueprint to show the vision for the NHS through 2028. It embedded goals for eradicating identified epidemics and implementing Integrated Care Systems to address ongoing health challenges within England.

7 — January 2019

Delayed response to COVID-19 pandemic
COVID-19 strikes the UK in January 2020. However, the primary policy response is inaction until March 2020 when illness rates reach historic levels. The lack of government preparation and reactions shifts priority funding and staffing to pandemic response – pausing aspects of the Long Term Plan.

March 2020 — 8

Figure 2.1: Timeline for English public health developments (continued)

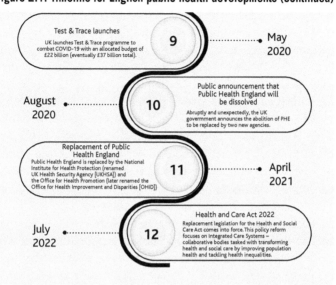

Public Health England

As part of the Lansley reforms affecting the whole health system and not only the NHS, public health was reformed both nationally and locally as set out in a White Paper, 'Healthy Lives, Healthy People' (Department of Health, 2010), and subsequently in the Health and Social Care Act 2012. PHE was established as an executive agency to provide national leadership for public health, while locally the lead responsibility for public health returned to local government, where it had been located prior to the 1974 NHS reorganisation. Although separate from the Department of Health (now the Department of Health and Social Care, DHSC) and organised into regional outposts, from the outset PHE lacked the independence accorded to some other national bodies, notably the National Institute for Health and Care Excellence (NICE). As a civil service agency rather than an arm's-length body, it remained part of the central DHSC.

Modelled largely on the Health Protection Agency which it replaced, PHE was given responsibility for two of the three domains of public health: health protection, including emergency preparedness, and health improvement (Griffiths et al, 2005). The third domain – health service quality improvement – remained with NHS England. Despite the formation of PHE, a sizeable public health group of civil servants remained located in the DHSC to service the public health minister and Chief Medical Officer (CMO) for England. This proved to be a major criticism of the public health reforms later levelled by the House of Commons Public Accounts Committee.

PHE's remit was focused on addressing public health challenges through influencing agendas by producing data, analysis and research; shaping policy and practice through evidence-informed solutions; delivering services through responding to health emergencies and public health campaigns; and building system capability through training, guidance and standards to deliver effective interventions. For instance, PHE led a work programme on Health in All Policies (HiAP) comprising a resource to support local authorities in their efforts to develop a collaborative approach to improving health (Connolly and PHE, 2016). Among PHE's strategic priorities for the period 2020–25, and set prior to its sudden abolition, foremost are a smoke-free society, healthier diets and weights, cleaner air, better mental health, and the best start in life (PHE, 2019). From this list of activities, it can be seen how broad and complex PHE's agenda was, especially in the light of what we shall see in this chapter was the squeeze on its funding and hence its limited capacity. It aspired to take on the broad agenda of public health that we identified in Chapter 1.

In a case study of health protection, the House of Commons Health Committee asserted that the system for health protection was more complicated than it was before 2013 (House of Commons Health Committee, 2016). It was argued by some witnesses that the separation of public health from the NHS had led to numerous difficulties including the sharing of, and access to, data on health protection incidents. A lot depended on goodwill. It was felt that this complexity and scale increased the chances of errors in communication and coordination occurring, and could cause delays in the response to outbreaks. At the same time, PHE regional centres were seen to be providing good support to local areas on health protection with the example given of the response to Ebola which had worked well. However, and presciently, when witnesses were asked how the new system would cope under the strain of a pandemic, they felt it would be more difficult than during the previous pandemic in 2009. In particular, concern was expressed over the reduced capacity and shrinking resources available since 2009, and the fact that people with experience and knowledge were no longer in post following the 2013 changes. PHE, in giving evidence, argued that some of the problems raised by witnesses around health protection responsibilities pre-dated the 2013 transfer to local authorities. It was aware that the guidance on outbreaks was not as clear as it needed to be, and that further work was needed on clarifying some of the roles and responsibilities, including improving clarity over funding arrangements.

However, not all observers have been as critical of PHE and its performance. As Vize records, PHE achieved a number of significant successes, including its work on Ebola in Sierra Leone, Guinea and Liberia, and on several public health challenges back in England (Vize, 2020). It was viewed as a model of best practice for other countries to follow. For example, the 2019 Global Health Security Index (2019: 20–21), a peer-led cross-national international assessment, placed the UK second (after the United States) among all countries surveyed for its general epidemic preparedness, gave it the top ranking on rapid response to and mitigation of an epidemic, and second place (again after the United States) on commitment to improving national capacity, financing and adherence to norms.

A study of institutionalising preventive health in three countries – Australia, New Zealand and England – commended PHE on its 'wily engagement with salient issues' (Boswell 2019: 207). Rather than attempt to 'speak truth to power', the researchers concluded that PHE 'has been careful to walk a fine line: upholding independence from government, but being careful not to lapse into preventive health "lobbying"' (Boswell et al, 2019: 208). The approach is described as one of 'muted advocacy', with PHE pursuing its agenda 'by stealth, building and leveraging good will with other powerful actors'. PHE's reputation, the researchers allege, was built by being viewed as independent 'knowledge brokers' thereby avoiding overt advocacy and a strong policy agenda. It is therefore claimed that PHE achieved widespread legitimacy through such means.

But while PHE's success as an institution may have been achieved, if the researchers' findings are upheld and to be believed, it does not necessarily equate with having achieved policy gains for the prevention agenda. It is on this issue that many in the wider public health community have been most critical of PHE's low-key approach and tendency to adopt controversial positions, notably in respect of its review of e-cigarettes, in which it claimed that they were 95% safer than traditional tobacco (PHE, 2015). Such a conclusion was met with considerable dismay, hostility and widespread opposition from many, though not all, in the public health community (Vize, 2020). It also pitted it against bodies such as WHO, which had concluded that e-cigarettes were far from safe.

PHE also came in for criticism in regard to its perceived proximity to the drinks industry following a decision to launch a health promotion partnership with Drinkaware, and for failing to be more critical of powerful commercial interests. Some observers saw PHE's approach to alcohol and tobacco as too focused on individual responsibility and behaviour change, thereby diverting attention from more effective policies such as minimum unit pricing (Gilmore et al, 2018). Arguably,

PHE's positioning on such matters may have been a result of the public health responsibility deal (RD) which was a feature of the Lansley reforms. The extent to which government should partner with business interests in order to improve public health is a much contested subject. One approach is to develop voluntary agreements with industry or allow them to self-regulate. The RD favoured by the coalition government and launched in 2011 entailed a public–private partnership and was organised around a series of voluntary agreements that sought to bring together government, academic experts, and commercial, public sector and voluntary bodies to commit to pledges to undertake actions of public health benefit. An evaluation of the RD by a team based at the London School of Hygiene and Tropical Medicine (LSHTM) concluded that it failed to meet its objectives since the pledges produced were largely driven by the interests of the partners, enabling the wider system to resist change (Knai et al, 2018).

The life of PHE coincided with the period of public sector austerity that was instituted by the Conservative-Liberal coalition government elected in 2010 and continued by the Conservative government elected in 2015. Spending on PHE fell in both real and nominal terms for virtually the whole period of its existence (Figure 2.2). Even when it rose in nominal terms at the end, it fell in real terms. One reason for the pressure on the PHE budget was that the claims of immediate spending on the NHS were politically more demanding. In his evidence to the UK Covid-19 Inquiry, the former head of PHE, Duncan Selbie, stated that the then Secretary of State for Health, Jeremy Hunt, wanted a 50 per cent cut to the public health budget to allocate to the NHS (Anderson, 2023).

Although the ostensible reason given for the abolition of PHE (see below) was its inability to scale up testing, it is clear that the money that eventually was allocated to Test and Trace was way beyond the annual budget for PHE. Indeed, it was some 60 times greater.

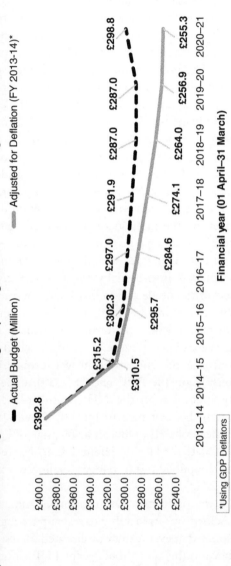

Figure 2.2: Public Health England annual budget. Spending allocation to PHE, excluding local authorities, 2014 to 2021

UK central government

As we saw in Chapter 1, one of the central challenges facing public health policy is that the achievement of public health aims requires intersectoral collaboration with other departments of state who may have different priorities. How successful was PHE in securing collaboration with other Whitehall departments? This question was examined by the House of Commons Public Accounts Committee (PAC) in its 2015 report, as well as by the House of Commons Health Committee.

In its report, the PAC concluded that PHE needed to influence central government departments more effectively and 'translate its own passion into action across Whitehall', a view subsequently shared by the House of Commons Health Committee, which concluded that PHE needed to do more work to ensure that all departments were on board with its priorities (House of Commons PAC, 2015: 3; House of Commons Health Committee, 2016)). Both the PAC and Health Committee expressed concern that PHE had been too timid, failing to speak truth to power (House of Commons Health Committee, 2014). Giving evidence to the PAC, PHE accepted that its work across government had not been as well coordinated or closely connected with its five priorities for health improvement as it should have been. PHE proposed that there should be a public health voice in major government departments and planned to address this through attaching regional directors of public health to major departments.

The Health Committee also considered that the relationship between the DHSC and PHE remained problematic and that PHE lacked the independence desired and expected of it (House of Commons Health Committee, 2014). In particular, it was concerned that there was insufficient separation between PHE and the Department of Health (DH). It concluded: 'PHE can only succeed if it is clear beyond doubt that its public statements and policy positions are not influenced by

Government policy or political considerations' (House of Commons Health Committee, 2014: paragraph 40). In its 2016 inquiry into public health post-2013, the Health Committee returned to the issue and noted that the interface between PHE and DH lacked clarity and urged the government to review the relationship between the DH's public health group and PHE. But the Committee located the DH–PHE relationship in a wider context of national system leadership, which was important to signal clarity of purpose and commitment to the local system when it came to improving health and well-being. It recommended that the government should produce a clear statement of who does what in respect of the main system leaders: namely DH, PHE and NHS England.

In its response to the Committee's report, the DH agreed that 'it would be helpful to review and optimise the relationship' between the Department and PHE (Department of Health, 2016: paragraph 11, p 9). In its defence, it also argued that the 2013 reforms 'deliberately avoided placing hard borders around the different components of the public health system' on the grounds that it would risk opening up 'stretches of no man's land between them as priorities evolve and new threats to health emerge' (Department of Health, 2016: paragraph 8, pp 7–8). Hence the emphasis in the reforms on encouraging partnerships and close collaboration between parts of the system, and that inevitably required a degree of overlap between what the national players may do. DH did not see this as a cause of confusion, although it acknowledged that there was some 'settling down' to be done in what is still 'a young system' (Department of Health, 2016: paragraph 8, pp 7–8).

PHE's lack of independence from government was viewed as especially problematic in the light of evidence that there had been political interference to suppress or delay the publication of reports, latterly in respect of some of its advice/guidance relating to COVID-19, but also in regard to some of its earlier preventive health work. This included a review of the evidence concerning sugar consumption and effects on obesity that proved to be critical of government policy, or rather the lack of one (Tedstone et al, 2015).

Other developments at national level included the launch of a Public Health Outcomes Framework (PHOF). First published in 2012 and reviewed every three years following consultation, it comprises five domains and a total of 159 indicators and subindicators covering the full spectrum of public health across the life course, locally and nationally, and what can realistically be measured. To strengthen and drive whole-of-government approaches to tackling the wider determinants of health, a cabinet subcommittee on public health under the Secretary of State for Health's leadership, similar to one that existed until 2012, was established to coordinate work across central departments. A new voluntary 'responsibility deal' was introduced, reflecting that private businesses and corporations should take more responsibility for the impact of their products and practices on health and well-being.

To be fair to PHE, securing effective cross-government working, previously referred to as joined-up government during the New Labour years, has never been easy or a priority for government, which remains heavily siloed, a common feature of organisations, as noted in Chapter 1. A study of joined-up government in tackling health inequalities concluded that it remained an aspiration rather than a reality with departmentalism firmly embedded (Exworthy and Hunter, 2011). There have been renewed calls for cross-sector working in government, and we return to these in the next chapter.

Local government

As well as establishing PHE, the Lansley reforms returned public health powers to local government, where they had originally been lodged until 1974. The vision was that localism was to be at the heart of the new system with responsibilities, freedoms and funding devolved wherever possible, especially to local government.

There has not been a great deal of completed research evaluating the public health changes since 2012, especially nationally. While the changes at local level, whereby the lead responsibility for public health was returned to local government from the NHS, have been generally well received (apart from the funding cuts over 13 years, which have hindered progress and contributed to the uncertainty around the priority accorded public health), at national level PHE has come in for mixed reviews and varying degrees of criticism.

Although the House of Commons PAC concluded that PHE 'has made a good start in its efforts to protect and improve public health', it felt that the organisation lacked 'strong enough ways of influencing local authorities to ensure progress against all of its top public health priorities' as measured against the PHOF (House of Commons PAC, 2015: 3). This followed the critical report from the National Audit Office (NAO), which was unimpressed with PHE's efforts to provide local authorities with evidence and decision support tools (NAO, 2014). Endorsing the criticism, the PAC recommended improved responsiveness on the part of PHE to local authority requests for support, including help with understanding the evidence base and cost implications of different public health interventions (NAO, 2014). To be fair to PHE, it could only seek to influence, and not direct, local authorities to make good progress in improving the public's health (Hunter, 2016). Such a limitation points to a tension that lay at the heart of PHE's remit. On the one hand, it was accountable for securing improved health outcomes but, on the other hand, the levers available to it to ensure that such outcomes were realised were few and limited in their reach. It is true that some public health functions are prescribed, and the DHSC can attach conditions to the PHE grant given to local authorities. But if the whole purpose and thrust of the changes and emphasis on localism was not to be rendered meaningless, it would not be appropriate to use such powers too often and for PHE to become overly directive in regard to local government. Such a move would have been fiercely resisted and hardly in the spirit of devolving responsibilities to locally elected bodies charged with determining their own priorities.

Compounding the dilemma was PHE's understandable desire to be the friend of local government – ready to support and assist it when required but reluctant to be perceived as an inspectorate wielding a big stick. As Buck concludes in his assessment of the public health reforms: 'PHE does not have a remit to police what local authorities choose to do, and beyond providing support and tools, intervenes only in ill-defined, exceptional circumstances. Into this gap, the main way that local government seeks to improve is through peer-to-peer improvement' (Buck, 2020). With the demise of the Audit Commission under the coalition government, whose role was to oversee local government performance, it is not self-evident how this central–local tension gets resolved, if indeed it can be beyond a 'muddling through' approach. In an effort to address the issue, the Local Government Association (LGA) has developed a sector-led improvement (SLI) approach based on the principle that the local government sector is responsible for its own improvement and how that is achieved through peer-to-peer challenge. The issue, as Buck notes, is whether SLI is sufficient for public health when the tools on offer are voluntary and make demands on hard-stretched local authorities (Buck, 2020). While SLI is of value and should continue, a key test for the new bodies that have replaced PHE will be the extent to which additional measures are required and, if they are, what form they will take in order to tackle variation among local authorities.

A similar tension between local autonomy and national policy was revealed in the conflict over funding that arose over pre-exposure prophylaxis (PrEP) in 2016. The background to this controversy was the effectiveness of Truvada, an antiretroviral treatment (ART) as PrEP, in the decline in new cases of HIV in key sexual health clinics in London (Tehseen et al, 2023). Used prophylactically, PrEP has been shown to reduce HIV infection by up to 86 per cent in the PROUD study (Pre-exposure Option for reducing HIV in the UK: immediate or deferred) (McCormack et al, 2016). The French multi-centre IPERGAY study also found an 86 per cent risk reduction in HIV incidence (Molina, 2015).

NHS England (NHSE) first set up the HIV Clinical Reference Group (CRG) to outline the policy for PrEP in September 2014. It commended the encouraging findings from the PROUD study and stated that it was the responsible commissioner for all ARTs (NHS England, 2016b). However, in March 2016, NHSE claimed that due to external legal advice, it did not have the power to commission PrEP (NHS England, 2016a). Given NHSE's previously positive assessment of PrEP, and the fact that PrEP is considered to be cost- and clinically effective (Cambiano et al. 2016), NHSE's standpoint led to bewilderment in the clinical and patient community. The justification for the decision was the Health and Social Care Act 2012, which transferred the responsibility for the treatment and prevention of sexually transmitted infections, including HIV, to local authorities. On this basis, NHSE argued that local authorities were the responsible commissioner for PrEP since it constituted a preventive strategy (NHS England, 2016a). The charity National AIDS Trust (NAT) sought a judicial review (supported by the local authorities) to challenge this decision, which it won in July 2016, and a subsequent appeal by NHSE was also lost. Rather than commissioning PrEP, NHSE agreed to support a three-year PrEP impact trial for 10,000 individuals that had recruited 3,200 participants as of January 2018.

The extent to which local authorities have been able to pursue public health initiatives has been limited by the extent to which their finance is dependent on grants from central government, which during the period since 2010 have been under considerable strain. The cuts to the public health grant have disproportionately fallen on some of the more deprived areas, such as Blackpool and other areas in the north and north east of England. But it is not just public health that has suffered. Local government as a whole has been hollowed out since 2010 and has borne the brunt of spending cuts introduced by austerity. The effect of COVID-19 has been to add further pressure on local authorities' finances, raising concerns about the sector's long-term financial sustainability (Murphie, 2023).

Importantly, local authorities provide a wide range of services that contribute to health and well-being. Between 2010 and 2017, government funding for local authorities halved. The impact of such deep cuts has meant that spending has become more narrowly focused on statutory responsibilities, such as social care, with other services falling behind (Lewer and Bibby, 2021). Services such as housing and treatment for drug and alcohol problems have been hardest hit, and yet they perform a crucial role in people's health and well-being. There is evidence to suggest that government funding cuts have had a direct impact on local authority-level mortality rates (Alexiou et al, 2021). The results show that areas with the biggest cuts to local government between 2013 and 2017 were associated with a reduction in national average life expectancy by about two months, equivalent to 96,000 premature deaths.

But there have been other setbacks. The impact of austerity has meant that a key *raison d'être* for relocating public health to local government has struggled to be realised. Local authorities may be regarded as public health organisations given that virtually all they are responsible for impacts on people's overall quality of life, health and well-being. Therefore, it was always intended that public health would work with, and influence the agendas of, other local authority services, thereby strengthening population health as a whole. While there have been some successes locally (for example in Wigan, Coventry and Manchester), these have been limited as a result of government funding policies.

Public health and the NHS

It has long been a commonplace that though named a health service, the NHS is largely an ill-health or sickness service, more concerned with treating disease and illness rather than preventing it or promoting health and well-being (Hunter, 2019). During the period when lead responsibility for public health resided with the NHS, between 1974 and 2013, that bias did not change despite successive attempts to confront it. The dilemma received particular attention in 2002, when Derek Wanless, appointed by the then Chancellor of the Exchequer, Gordon Brown, to investigate whether the NHS could survive as a tax-funded service beyond 2022, reiterated what many observers had been saying for years (Wanless, 2002). Wanless concluded his review by insisting that the NHS's survival depended crucially on the extent to which it could be rebalanced to attach a higher priority to prevention and public health. Only in doing so could the NHS meet the growing demands on it arising from largely avoidable and preventable lifestyle-related illnesses. Crucially, however, Wanless underlined the extent to which effective preventive action required government action. A reliance on individual behaviour change would not suffice. In his 'fully engaged scenario', which the government signed up to at the time, Wanless argued that its attainment depended on the extent to which greater priority was attached to public health. He returned to this theme in a follow-up report when he opined that public health remained a victim of a persistent policy dilemma which had yet to be resolved (Wanless, 2004).

The argument resurfaced in 2014 in the 'Five Year Forward View', in which the newly appointed NHS chief executive, Simon Stevens, revisited Wanless's critique (NHS England, 2014). The review opened with an indictment of the government's failure to commit to the fully engaged scenario and for not having heeded Wanless's warning that the sustainability of the NHS 'depends on a radical upgrade in prevention and public health' (NHS England, 2014: paragraphs 3 and 4, p 4). Building on this thinking, which was novel for the NHS, the 'NHS Long Term Plan' (LTP), published in 2019, devoted a whole chapter to prevention and health inequalities (NHS Executive, 2019). It was unprecedented for an NHS strategy to devote so much attention to these issues. Among various topics, the plan noted the need for action on smoking, obesity, alcohol, air pollution and health inequalities. It also carried a lengthy appendix detailing the NHS's support for wider social goals in regard to employment, and viewing NHS bodies as 'anchor institutions' in local communities.

At its core, the LTP set out a new service model for the 21st century centred on five major practical changes, three of which are especially relevant to our focus on public health. They are:

- Boosting 'out of hospital' care, including dissolving the historic divide between primary and community health services
- Reducing pressure on, and admission to, emergency hospital services
- Local NHS organisations increasingly focused on population health and local partnerships with local authority-funded services through new integrated care systems (ICSs).

The intention behind the creation of ICSs was to give the NHS a population-level perspective on health policy. They are charged with strengthening population health and tackling health inequalities as two of their four key aims. With the passage of the Health and Care Act 2022, 42 ICSs have been established, and their evolving progress, and the challenges facing them, are reviewed in our final chapter.

As we noted in Chapter 1, the Hewitt Review revisits many of these arguments. Yet still, over two decades after Wanless, the focus of policy makers' attention continues to be on the NHS as a sickness, and not a health, service. Politicians, the public and media often collude to keep the focus on waiting lists and times, elective care backlogs, the need for more hospitals and beds, and so on. These become the enduring priorities when it comes to funding decisions, with budgets skewed towards treating sick people rather than keeping people well. The desire for a population-level perspective was also a driver for relocating public health locally to local government from the NHS in 2013. But unsurprisingly, in view of public expenditure cuts and the policy focus on the NHS, public health in local authorities often did not get the priority it merited. Indeed, there were instances of raids on public health budgets by the then Primary Care Trusts in order to balance the books and keep acute services solvent – a move much criticised by the CMO for England at the time, Liam Donaldson. Such pressures have become even greater as a result of COVID-19, which has contributed to the growing backlog of elective care.

Summing up this story of public health and the NHS, we see that in place of what should be a complementary relationship between public health and the NHS, there is a competitive relationship. Only public health measures can reduce the demand on NHS services, the failure to meet that demand being the cause of the intense public and political focus on the NHS. But the priority given to short-term funding fixes for the NHS undercuts the priority for public health. There is a doom loop built into the policy process: failure to act vigorously on public health increases the demands on the NHS; the short-term financial fixes to meet that demand become inevitable in the light of public concern; those short-term fixes undercut the funding and priority given to public health; the failure to address the public health challenges increases the demand on NHS services. And so the loop continues.

Turning points

In August 2020 the UK government without warning announced the abolition of PHE. It was to be merged with the recently formed Test and Trace service and the Joint Biosecurity Centre to form a new agency, eventually named the UK Health Security Agency (UKHSA). UKHSA went on subsequently to absorb the Vaccine Task Force that had been established during the COVID-19 pandemic to oversee the procurement of vaccines. Another new body, eventually named the Office for Health Improvement and Disparities (OHID), was created to take on responsibility for health promotion that had previously been lodged with PHE. However, rather than being established as an executive agency, like UKHSA, OHID formed a directorate in the DHSC.

The decision to abolish PHE was controversial, both at the time and subsequently, with leading health policy experts questioning the timing and wisdom of the decision. Richard Murray, former chief executive of the King's Fund, said that 'the middle of a pandemic is not the time to dismantle England's public health agency', and Nigel Edwards, former chief executive of the Nuffield Trust, said that 'the government risks making a major misstep by dismantling its own public health agency at such a crucial time'. What is more, PHE had shown its scientific mettle early in the pandemic when it was able quickly to establish a test for infection by the COVID-19 virus, particularly important for a disease that could be transmitted asymptomatically. There was, then, a widespread sense in the health policy community that PHE was being scapegoated for the failures and delays of government policy in the pandemic (for an account, see Weale et al, 2023).

The reason given for the sudden reorganisation was the failure of PHE to be able to scale up testing and tracing. In a speech shortly after the announcement, the Secretary of State for Health and Social Care at the time, Matt Hancock, said:

'We can learn from countries like South Korea and Germany's Robert Koch Institute, where their health protection agencies have a huge primary focus on

pandemic response. We will build the same focus here.'
(Cited in Iacobucci, 2020)

The promise of the Secretary of State was that the reorganisation would mark a decisive improvement in the UK's capacity to ensure health security and so public health more generally.

However, there is a case to be made that the failure of the UK's public health system adequately to prepare and respond to COVID-19 was not the fault of one agency, a fault that could be remedied by a limited piece of organisational redesign, but was rather a particular manifestation of a more general feature of UK government and governance. Writing of the UK government's 2021 Integrated Review of Security, Lord Ricketts (2021: x–xi) said that the review 'gave no clear sense of what government actually plans to do. Indeed it left the suspicion that there is no real strategy, beyond setting out bold aspirations in all directions and then continuing to muddle through'. The same logic of muddling through was exemplified in the creation of UKHSA since, *after the decision to abolish PHE had been taken*, the consulting firm McKinsey 'was paid more than half a million pounds by the UK government for six weeks of work to decide the "vision, purpose and narrative" of a new public health authority in England' (Kinder, 2020). In other words, the rhetoric of reform was unaccompanied by the practicalities of realistic planning, giving rise to the suspicion that the reorganisation itself was a piece of blame-shifting behaviour based on the well-known principle of 'find a scapegoat' by defensive reorganisation (see Weale et al, 2023).

By this reckoning, the policy failures around COVID-19 are part of a broader pattern of UK governance in which public health, and the common good of which public health is such a central part, have been neglected. Ultimately, we shall argue, we need a new social contract that places at its centre precautionary principles and concern for the common good shared by citizens of equal standing. Only then will health policy be truly public.

Before we reach that conclusion, however, we need to consider in more detail the policy and organisational challenges of public health itself, since the lesson of public health reform in the UK is that aspirational goals need to be joined with realistic understanding of how institutions function. How should we think about the organisational design, policy paradigm and public philosophy that makes for effective, reliable and robust public health policy? One of our central assumptions in this regard is that policy makers need to think about the organisations that formulate and implement public health measures *as a system*. A reform like the abolition of PHE and its replacement by UKHSA and OHID creates a new set of relationships with the NHS, local government and the devolved governments of the home nations. As Hunter et al (2010, chapter 2) pointed out over a decade ago, a public health system, when fully mapped, will include not only government bodies, but also employers and businesses, the media, academia and communities of various sorts. In this book we cannot map this full system, but we can look at how public health is organised in the home nations, a task to which we turn in the next chapter.

THREE

Public health and
the devolved governments

Introduction

In the previous chapter we saw how Public Health England (PHE) was the product of the Lansley broader reforms of the NHS, reforms that also included the return of public health functions to local government. A notable feature of the transformation of the UK since 1998 has been the extension and devolution of powers from Westminster and Whitehall to Scotland, Wales and Northern Ireland. Devolution means that in areas of policy that are not reserved to the UK government, which in health policy are very few, the governments of the home nations have the freedom to determine their own policies, priorities and structures. This has been notably true in the provision of health care services, where the Welsh, Scottish and Northern Ireland governments have opted for greater stability in place of successive structural reforms, and have not made competition and performance management a central guiding principle as the UK government has done to an increasing degree since the Thatcher reforms. However, the distinctiveness has also shown up in public health policies and structures.

Looking at public health in the devolved governments is important for a number of reasons, quite apart from the simple need to avoid Anglo-centrism. In the first place, the organisation of public health in the devolved governments provides interesting points of similarity and difference to those in England. If the replacement of PHE took place without any forethought, the same is not true in the other home nations where, in keeping with health care services, there has been great stability of organisation, alongside policy developments. So patterns of structural organisation provide interesting evidence of the various ways in which public health functions can be organised. As we shall see in this chapter, there is no one uniform set of functions that are the responsibility of the public health bodies. Functions that are the responsibility of a public health agency in one of the home nations may be the responsibility of, say, the environment agency of another home nation.

Variation in the home nations in the organisation of public health also potentially poses another challenge to effective public health. If public health requires intersectoral collaboration across government, the conduct of policy in the UK requires collaboration across the governments of the home nations. Although the United Kingdom Health Security Agency (UKHSA) has responsibilities for reserved health matters within the UK's devolution settlement, its main responsibilities relate to England. The experience of COVID-19 was that different governments in the UK could adopt different policies in respect of restrictions on movement and social mixing. Night clubs might be open in Bristol, for example, but not in Cardiff, even though someone living in Bristol might work in Cardiff. The policy question to which this sort of example leads concerns how responsibility for different areas of policy should be assigned to different home nations' governments.

In themselves, differences of policies should not be problematic. Indeed, the variation that they create should be an opportunity for finding different solutions to complex problems leading to policy learning. For example, the Welsh decision to move from explicit to presumed consent in respect of organ donation, or the Scottish government's pursuit of minimum unit pricing for alcohol provide evidence of the effects of policies from which others can learn. How far such opportunities are taken is a different matter, however. An important part of public health policy ought to be to learn from such evidence, despite the problems of transferring policy learning from one jurisdiction to another.

Devolved governments

All the home nations now have designated public health bodies. Wales and Northern Ireland established their agencies in 2009, with Public Health Wales and the Public Health Agency in Northern Ireland. Scotland is a relative latecomer in terms of organisation, with Public Health Scotland only being established in 2020. However, in some respects, namely minimum unit pricing of alcohol and the first smoking ban in public places, Scotland offers two of the most distinctive policy initiatives, a reminder that organisational structures are only part of the policy story. In this section we survey the developments distinctive to each government.

Wales

Wales pursued the most radical attempt to shift the focus of health care away from hospital and GP provision and towards public health (Greer, 2008: 3). There was initially a focus on localism and an attempt to attack the wider social determinants of health, with a reorganisation in 2003 which brought health boards and local government into alignment. Wales was also early in establishing a separate national public health agency, Public Health Wales (PHW), which has a wide range of responsibilities including those that elsewhere are seen as parts of environmental protection.

PHW has pursued health impact assessments as one of its distinctive approaches. Obviously, it is difficult to know what impact they might have, but at least the very act of conducting such assessments offers an attempt to make public the implications of particular government actions or inactions.

The first initiative concerns the Well-being of Future Generations (Wales) Act 2015. This creates a statutory duty for public bodies to demonstrate how policies impact a number of areas, including health (https://phwwhocc.co.uk/whiasu/hia-reports/).

The second initiative relates to the Wales Health Impact Assessment Support Unit, which has done extensive analysis on the health impacts of Brexit, COVID-19, and the lockdowns among other things (https://phwwhocc.co.uk/whiasu/news/). PHW has also called for a health impact assessment of the Comprehensive and Progressive Agreement on Trans-Pacific Partnership (CPTPP) which is seen to pose a threat to health (McNamara et al, 2023).

The long-term strategy of Public Health Wales (2023) for 2023 to 2035 identifies six priorities, which are set in the context of need to work collaboratively across organisations. The priorities of the strategy are intended to reflect the particular health care circumstances and profile of the Welsh population, including an ageing population and wide health inequalities. They are set out in six broad themes: influencing the wider determinants of health; promoting mental health well-being; promoting healthy behaviour; supporting the delivery of a sustainable health and care system; delivering excellent public health services; and tackling the public health effects of climate change. The overarching theme is the attempt to reduce health inequalities.

Northern Ireland

Northern Irish policy development since the Good Friday agreement has been limited in part as a consequence of long periods of time during which the Assembly has not met because of its being boycotted by one or other of the political parties, and also in part due to the veto points built into the policy system by the system of consociational democracy that the Good Friday agreement created. As a result, some policies have been a consequence of direct rule from Westminster. In principle, the brigading of health and social care in the Health and Social Care territorial boards should give a more holistic approach to health care, but how far this is so is unclear. Like Wales, Northern Ireland did acquire a dedicated public health body, the Public Health Agency in 2009.

Scotland

Scotland, too, diverged from the English model of competitive organisation and was early with some important public health initiatives, including the banning of smoking in public places and the introduction of minimum unit pricing for alcohol, the latter reflecting its greater tax-raising powers than other devolved governments.

Scotland faces three major public health challenges:

- relatively poor health (compared with the rest of Western Europe);
- significant and persistent inequalities in health outcomes;
- unsustainable pressures on health and social care services.

Like Wales, Scotland centralised the public health function into a separate agency, initially NHS Health Scotland (Greer, 2016: 21). However, acknowledging that Scotland's public health approach was failing to deliver improvement in these areas, the Scottish government and the Convention of Scottish Local Authorities (COSLA) decided to set up a new national body, Public Health Scotland (PHS). The new single body brought Scotland into line with the rest of the UK, at least until PHE was abolished. It was felt that bringing together national public health information and intelligence, health protection and health improvement expertise and knowledge into a single body would improve coordination and give a stronger voice than any single part of the system operating in isolation.

Importantly, the focus from the start was on taking a whole-systems approach engaging all key stakeholder groups, with PHS jointly accountable to the Scottish government and to local government via COSLA to ensure more effective connection between national and local work to improve the public's health. An emphasis was placed on working with communities to develop local solutions to local public health challenges. There was also emphasis on tackling the wider social and economic determinants of health.

During the two years PHS was in development, public health reform was overseen by a Public Health Reform Programme Board set up in 2017. To help create PHS, the reform programme invited 'think pieces' on various aspects of Scotland's public health from people across the system. Analysis of the material led to the Public Health Reform Programme Board asking partnerships from existing public health organisations and other members of the public health system to lead a series of commissions and projects. Their purpose was to inform the design of PHS so that it was best placed to meet the ambitions of public health reform.

Eight commissions were set up covering the following topics:

- improving services
- improving health
- leadership for public health research, innovation and applied evidence
- leadership for public health workforce
- organisational development
- protecting health
- underpinning data and intelligence
- specialist public health workforce

Throughout 2018 and early 2019 the commissions met, took evidence from hundreds of people who attended stakeholder events across the country, and captured the opinions of others through a survey. Each commission reported against a number of defined deliverables and made recommendations on how the relevant functions of PHS should operate. The final reports from the commissions and projects were aggregated into a Target Operating Model which provided the basis for establishing PHS.

One of us (Hunter) chaired the commission on Leadership for Public Health Research, Innovation and Applied Evidence and therefore had first-hand experience of, and involvement in, the public health reform process. He is therefore able to testify to its depth, rigour and the detailed work undertaken to ensure that PHS was established on firm foundations and with the support of key stakeholders in the public health system. The process involved considerable energy and commitment on the part of those leading the commissions.

It is early days and only time will tell if PHS can meet the significant and complex challenges it is tasked with addressing. But what stands out from its formation was the extensive programme of work undertaken in its preparation and launch – in striking contrast to what happened in England following the sudden abolition of PHE and its hasty (some would say over-hasty) replacement by two new bodies.

Mapping public health functions comparatively

How functions are allocated among different bodies is a question in public administration. We have identified one of the central challenges of public health as being intersectoral collaboration. How does a public health body collaborate with a transport body or a housing body or a competition body? However, there is a prior question, which concerns the extent to which public bodies labelled as being about public health monopolise the functions of public health. After all, the regulation of environmental or workplace hazards is a health task, but the responsibility for monitoring drinking water quality may not lie with the public health body, and the regulation of workplace safety may fall to an agency specialising in that field.

The comparison of the allocation of functions to the public health bodies of the home nations is instructive in this regard, enabling us to see the various ways in which functions can be allocated. In examining those differences across the UK, we have drawn data from the publicly available sources on the websites of the UKHSA, Public Health Scotland, Public Health Wales, and the Public Health Agency in Northern Ireland, all of which list the scope of their responsibilities. Figure 3.1 shows the division of public health responsibilities across these bodies in the UK. Helpfully, UKHSA categorises its 215 responsibilities into four broad groups – exposure to chemicals, environmental health hazards, health emergencies, and infectious disease control – and we have followed this categorisation for all the home nations' bodies. Some of these responsibilities are shared by all four bodies; some are shared by fewer; and others fall just to one body. Figure 3.1 shows how this sharing of responsibilities varies by topic, with a much greater concentration of responsibility for chemicals, for example, by comparison with emergency response or infectious diseases.

Figure 3.2 provides some detail about how these responsibilities are distributed across the four bodies. The contrast between infectious diseases and chemicals is most striking. A large number of health hazards are included in each of these two categories. In the case of infectious diseases, the vast majority of the diseases fall within the responsibility of all four bodies. By contrast, UKHSA has responsibility for most of the chemical hazards.

An important implication of the same responsibility being shared among different organisations is that interorganisational

Figure 3.1: Categorisation of public health responsibilities

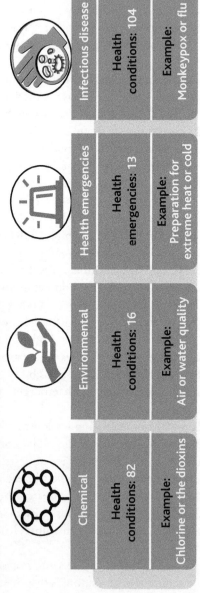

Chemical

Health conditions: 82

Example: Chlorine or the dioxins

Environmental

Health conditions: 16

Example: Air or water quality

Health emergencies

Health emergencies: 13

Example: Preparation for extreme heat or cold

Infectious disease

Health conditions: 104

Example: Monkeypox or flu

Figure 3.2: Distribution of public health responsibilities

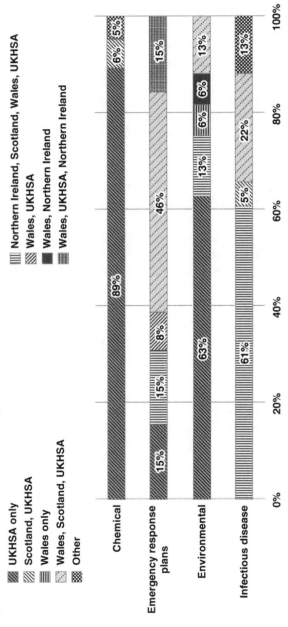

collaboration becomes important. When a new organisation is created, people often draw attention to the need to meld together the different cultural orientations of its different components, as has happened with bringing together Test and Trace and PHE in the new UKHSA. This is obviously a major challenge. However, given that health hazards do not recognise administrative and political boundaries, it is just as important that a territorially based organisation be able to work with similar territorially based organisations in other jurisdictions. For example, the UKHSA provided advice to the Chief Medical Officers (CMOs) in UK jurisdictions on the level of the COVID-19 alert in late May 2022. (See https://www.gov.uk/government/news/uk-covid-alert-level.)

From one point of view, having separate organisations can lead to inconsistencies, as happened in the pandemic when, at times, different advice was issued in respect of travel, meetings and leisure. However, policy learning is also possible. Organisational differences can be examined to see whether they make a difference to policy effectiveness. Are health hazards from water pollution dealt with any differently in Wales, where Public Health Wales has some responsibility for water contaminants, as distinct from Scotland, where water pollution is the responsibility of the Scottish Environmental Protection Agency? We know of no systematic programme to monitor and analyse these sorts of differences, although an understanding of their effects would be a potentially valuable source of policy learning.

Against this background, it should not be surprising that the conduct of organisational interrelationships becomes important. There is an established practice of the CMOs of the home nations working together, and we have seen the role that PHE played in the support of local government. The remit of UKHSA brings home how extensive are the tasks associated with organisational interrelationships, with UKHSA being charged with working together with Public Health Wales, Public Health Scotland and other bodies.

A wider problem is the absence of a forum in which such lesson-learning can take place. Possible forums do exist and to a degree fill a gap, notably the UK Public Health Forum and the People in UK Public Health forum, but to date they have tended to be topic-based rather than providing opportunities to learn systematically across the devolved arrangements.

Common challenges, different organisations

The creation of a new governmental body like UKHSA can give the impression that the reform of a single organisation should be the focus of improving the machinery of government in respect of public health. However, the above account of the variety of organisations with responsibility for public health shows that, when seeking to understand the functioning of public health policy, we should really think of a public health system, a set of different bodies whose choices and behaviour interact with one another, rather than of one particular organisation, like UKHSA, no matter how strategically important that organisation is.

Moreover, there is no reason to expect consistency across the home nations in the way that functions are assigned to the principal public health body in government. In some parts of the UK, a hazard will be the responsibility of the public health body but in others the responsibility, for example, of an environment agency. Thus, in Wales drinking water falls to the remit of PHW, whereas in Scotland it falls to the remit of the Scottish Environmental Protection Agency. Different national governments will have different organisational arrangements for their various departments; and sometimes an already existing agency, like the Scottish Environmental Protection Agency, will have established a track record in a particular area of concern. This variety of organisational forms should undermine the assumption that there is one 'best' way of assigning functions to bodies. Much depends on context, history and the scale of resources that are available. Given the complex nature of the tasks that confront public health governance, as well as the constraints on institutional design that overarching constitutional arrangements impose, there is no one blueprint for the design of effective public health organisations. Moreover, even the best-designed organisational structure will fail if decision-makers within it are not able to pursue their policies through accountable practices.

However, there is one qualification to scepticism about there being one right organisational form for public health. All the public health agencies of the home nations, with the exception of England, brigade health protection and health promotion together. In this respect the separation of functions between UKHSA and OHID is an outlier.

Conclusions

We started by noting that there was something important to be learned about the allocation of public health functions to different organisations from a comparison of the responsibilities of public health bodies in the home nations of the UK. What should be apparent from our analysis is that there is no one-to-one correspondence between public health effectiveness and any particular way of assigning functions. Giving the public health body more functions will not of itself improve effectiveness. What matters instead is the ability to forge good policy relationships with those bodies that have adjacent or relevant responsibilities, against the incentives to silo thinking.

The example of Scotland provides one more lesson. The two major health initiatives in Scotland, the ban on smoking in public places and minimum unit pricing for alcohol, took place before the creation of PHS. Their adoption did not depend on how precisely the public health functions were allocated to governmental bodies. Rather it depended on a high-level political commitment to pursue the policies, sometimes against well-organised opposition. There were, of course, constitutional prerequisites, not least in the case of minimum unit pricing the Scottish government's tax-varying powers, which is an important policy instrument that other devolved governments lack. But though organisation is important, high-level political commitment is vitally important.

FOUR

Principles and process in the new public health settlement

Introduction

As we saw in the previous two chapters, the UK now has a new public health settlement. As far as England is concerned, in place of Public Health England (PHE), there are now two bodies, the UK Health Security Agency (UKHSA), with primary responsibility for health protection, and the Office for Health Improvement and Disparities (OHID), with primary responsibility for health promotion. (UKHSA also has responsibility for non-devolved health matters for the whole of the UK.) In addition, the administrative structure of the NHS has been altered with the establishment of integrated care systems (ICSs) intended to bring together local authorities, the NHS and other agencies with the intention of taking a population-based perspective. The one part of the original 2013 Lansley reforms that survived these changes concerns the public health responsibilities of local authorities.

The English reforms have been high-profile changes. Developments in Scotland, Wales and Northern Ireland, while significant, have largely involved a concentration of public health responsibilities over time as part of planned changes to administrative arrangements. In each case, however, the direction of change is the opposite of what has occurred in England. Instead of a separation of health protection and health promotion, the devolved governments have created integrated bodies. These bodies still have to liaise with local government, but they do so from a position in which public health can be seen as a set of overall responsibilities.

This chapter focuses on the policy and process issues to which these new structures give rise. The Hancock reforms, like many machinery of government changes, underline the point that, in some circumstances, organisational arrangements become the prime object of policy. Reorganisation provides a way of deflecting blame and also a way of seeming to make a new start quickly and visibly. Moreover, machinery of government changes are attractive to high-level political representatives, since they signal interest in an area of policy without the need to go into detail about any one aspect of policy. Thus, the political attraction of reorganisation is that it makes the politician play the role of God in eighteenth-century Christian theology, whose responsibility was to create the system that would then look after itself, according to its own laws. However, successful policy must go beyond the establishment of new organisations. Administrative organisations need to be imbued with purpose, becoming instruments of substantive policy, not the objects of policy in themselves.

UKHSA and OHID

UKHSA is an executive agency, with the independence that this status gives, although it is ultimately accountable to the Secretary of State. By contrast, OHID sits within the Department of Health and Social Care (DHSC). At the time of writing, the internal organisation of UKHSA is not fully complete, as the Vaccines Task Force is in process of being integrated into the organisation. However, the principal points of organisation seem clear, in particular that UKHSA is responsible for health protection, while OHID is responsible for health promotion. This separation of functions and organisations prompts two issues. Firstly, does the separation of health protection and health promotion make sense in itself? Secondly, accepting that there are two separate organisations, does the fact that OHID sits within the department mean that it is likely to be less independent and therefore less robust in terms of the policies that it can pursue and promote than it would be if it had the status of an executive agency?

Turning to the first of these questions, one of the widely applauded aspects of the Lansley reforms was the union of health promotion and health protection in PHE as one organisation, a coming together of responsibilities that the rest of the UK has followed, most recently Public Health Scotland. Issues of smoking, alcohol consumption or obesity were no longer separated from issues of health protection. In some ways this could be regarded as an aspect of the Faculty of Public Health's definition of health improvement, which is seen to be much wider than simply regarding issues like smoking and excessive alcohol consumption, as expressions of 'lifestyle' choices. The creation of two new organisations, UKHSA and OHID, administratively separates the domains again and raises issues about collaboration and cross-agency working similar to those which preceded PHE.

However, in terms of the management of public health problems, there is no clear separation of health protection and health promotion. The significance of this relationship was brought out during the COVID-19 pandemic. As Richard Horton (2020) has written, COVID-19 is not a pandemic to be managed purely on the model of transmissible disease control but interacts as a syndemic with non-communicable diseases, so that addressing COVID-19 'means addressing hypertension, obesity, diabetes, cardiovascular and chronic respiratory diseases, and cancer'. Since health disparities and inequalities arise through the interaction of biological and social processes, the proper management of a disease like COVID-19 entails looking at these broader forces operating on the health of the population. A similar point can be made in respect of air pollution. Exposure to the health risks of urban air pollution has a clear social gradient, which means that OHID has an interest given its brief on 'disparities'. However, understanding the pathways by which urban air pollutants adversely affect health is a matter of health protection.

The danger of separating health protection and health promotion is that of silo thinking. Organisational routines play a large part in shaping operational thinking, so it is perfectly possible that two organisations will fragment understanding of a problem rather than integrate thinking in a synoptic way. During periods of public expenditure constraint, the likelihood of organisations working to their own priorities is stronger. It may well be that good interorganisational collaboration can overcome this problem of fragmentation. It is possible to imagine, for example, that for a problem like air pollution UKHSA could provide the basis of scientific understanding of the effects of air pollution in biological terms, while OHID traced out the implications for social inequalities. However, if something like a well-functioning division of labour between the organisations is to be established, the respective remits of UKHSA and OHID need to be clearer and more transparent. Because of the circumstances in which both organisations were developed, as well as the political instabilities of the Johnson government and its successors, the remit of OHID in particular is only partially developed, not helped by the government's decision to abandon publication of its long-awaited White Paper on tackling health inequalities. For example, when we were undertaking our research workshops on the demise of PHE, one participant pointed out that early in its existence some staff denied that it had responsibility for air pollution. That situation has now changed, but exactly how responsibility on this and other issues will be shared between OHID and UKHSA is something that is likely to be worked out on an issue-by-issue basis.

Uncertainty as to the responsibilities of the two bodies leads on to our second question of the independence of OHID, given that it is now a part of government. The concern here is that health promotion has been brought in-house because, particularly with the libertarian wing of the Conservative Party, it is politically controversial. There have been some occasions in the past when health protection has proved to be politically controversial: for example, with salmonella in eggs, and BSE. However, health promotion has more regularly been a thorn in the side of governments. In the 1980s the Health Education Council was eventually abolished by the Thatcher government because it was regarded as an irritant, given that its independent status made it difficult for the government to control it. It was replaced in 1987 with the Health Education Authority, constituted as a special health authority and making it more accountable to ministers. But disputes with government continued and it also came close to being abolished. In the end, ministers proposed a contract-based system of funding that reduced its freedom. Against this background, one way of interpreting the creation and location of OHID is that its operating within the DHSC will make it more difficult to raise politically difficult issues as PHE did, for example, over the minimum unit pricing of alcohol.

Rather different, if related, issues arise in the case of UKHSA. Although as an executive agency it is more independent of day-to-day government, the scope of the policy remit is set by the Secretary of State for Health and Social Care through an annual 'remit letter', the first one of which was published in August 2022 (DHSC, 2022b). In the first remit letter, the priorities broadly specified, and are divided into, three groups: reducing harm from infectious diseases and other health security hazards; preparing for future health security hazards; and strengthening health security capacity. Within these broad categories, the items mentioned cover what might be expected from anyone who has followed the public health agenda in recent years. Reducing harm from infectious diseases covers action not only in relation to COVID-19, but also tuberculosis, antimicrobial resistance and sexually transmitted infections, alongside air pollution. A notable feature of the priorities is the emphasis on developing the capacity to scale up testing for COVID-19, a role that reflects the incorporation of Test and Trace into the same organisation. In addition, given the anchoring of UKHSA in the scientific expertise that was a feature of PHE, the organisation is given a role in supporting research in the life sciences.

The framework document for UKHSA identifies scientific integrity and independence in the delivery of policy advice as key elements in the mandate for the executive agency. Public confidence is also said to rest on accountability and ministerial oversight. In this chapter we examine the meaning of these ideas. We suggest, in particular, that the concept of scientific integrity is complex in a context in which health problems are rooted in social systems and in which uncertainties are pervasive. Nonetheless, some form of scientific integrity is important if public accountability is to be maintained. In turn, this requirement leads on to the conditions for securing independence in the giving of policy advice, particularly when that advice may be unpalatable to ministers.

There is no comparable framework document for OHID, but our analysis of scientific integrity and accountability would apply across the public health system, even allowing for the fact that as part of DHSC, OHID stands in a different institutional relationship to ministers. Political turbulence during the summer of 2022 seems to have inhibited development of a corresponding set of priorities for OHID itself, though its public statement (OHID, 2021) identifies its role in broad terms as building scientific evidence around such issues as healthy weight, healthy diet and physical activity, improving the health of children and families, smoking addiction, the health of vulnerable groups, and mental health. OHID's own statement says that it aims to provide evidence for 'the effective delivery of prevention services, helping individuals to better understand and manage their health'.

Scientific integrity

The framework document for UKHSA says that its strategic aims are to anticipate threats to health and build health security using 'cutting edge environmental and biological surveillance to proactively detect and monitor infectious diseases and threats to health' as well as using 'world-class science and data analytics to assess and continually monitor threats to health, identifying how best to control and mitigate the risks' (DHSC, 2022a: paragraph 2.5, p 8). At this level of abstraction, these aims are of course unexceptionable. No one is going to favour using second-rate science or a haphazard approach to monitoring threats as an aim of a public agency. However, in trying to spell out what scientific integrity might mean in this context, complexities arise.

It is tempting to equate scientific integrity with the study of biomedical systems as the 'hard core' of the relevant science. However, even in connection with dose-response relationships, there can be disputes about the effects of exposure to pollutants, as there has been in the case of air pollution, for example (Atkinson et al, 2013). Moreover, judgements about the effectiveness of a vaccine programme will need to take into account issues of vaccine hesitancy, and judgements about the risk of extreme weather events will need to take into account responses in terms of risk perception.

The need for a broad concept of evidence is particularly applicable in the field of health promotion. Public health problems arise in the 'open system' of social factors that predispose individuals to certain diseases. As Rutter et al (2017) suggest, a complex systems model of public health 'conceptualises poor health and health inequalities as outcomes of a multitude of interdependent elements within a connected whole'. Rutter et al give the example of obesity, which can be regarded as an emergent property of a series of systems – including employment, transport and economic elements, as well as systems of food supply – that affect the energy intake and expenditure of individuals. Another example would be the health effects of air pollution, which in part depend on the susceptibility of individuals to airborne chemicals, but the exposure itself depends on housing location, transport systems, industrial activity and weather patterns. Whereas clinical trials use an experimental method to abstract from context, a whole-systems approach locates the sources of ill health as operating within different types of social systems.

Thus, public health policy making necessarily requires drawing on a wide range of different types of evidence in a practical context in which decisions have to be made and where delaying a decision is itself a decision. Delaying a decision until the underpinning evidence reaches the highest standards of peer review risks allowing serious problems to continue. There is a potential tension between the high hurdles needed for peer review and the availability of evidence required for decision-making in policy. The system of peer review publishing, rightly from the point of view of the integrity of science, is biased against novel results, making it hard to overturn established opinion unless there are strong reasons to do so. In this way, purely hypothetical claims do not enter the canon of accepted evidence. But the integrity of science as a system of hypothesis testing does not sit easily alongside the need for policy action on suspected risks, where lack of action is itself a policy.

These problems have been known for a long time. In the 1980s, those concerned about lead in the atmosphere faced this problem. Evidence of harmful health effects from lead in the atmosphere of a standard that would pass the test of stringent peer review was not available. When the Royal Commission on Environmental Pollution discussed the question, some of its members saw their role as counselling against too demanding a concept of evidence:

'[T]here were scientists, I think, who were constantly aware that the kinds of recommendations we were making could not stand up to the scrutiny of [their] peers ... and the evidence was very shaky ... [M]y role was partly to say we can't expect [the] level of proof that would absolutely satisfy because we can't set up controls, we can't do any of the things that you do if you were conducting a proper scientific programme.' (Quoted in Owens, 2015: 84)

In recent years, similar disagreements have arisen about the precise relationships between various types of air pollutants, with Atkinson et al (2013) suggesting that particulates and NO_x were related to heart failure, but not to the wide range of cardiovascular outcomes suggested in the report of the Royal College of Physicians (2016).

However, even if the scale and significance of the problems are understood, it may be hard to establish firm evidence about the effects of particular policy interventions. Even if policy makers have a good understanding of the causes of ill health, it does not follow that they can reliably predict what the effects of a policy intervention might be. It may be relatively easy to estimate the health effects of ethanol consumption, but hard to estimate the response in terms of the consumption of drinkers to a change in price. Rising alcohol consumption may be creating long-term health effects, but what the most effective interventions might be involves practical judgement about policy instruments.

The need to draw on a wide range of evidence is illustrated by the controversy originally prompted by PHE's decision to support the use of e-cigarettes. In its review of e-cigarettes, PHE claimed that they were 95% safer than traditional tobacco (PHE, 2015). Such a conclusion was met with considerable dismay, hostility and widespread opposition from many, though not all, in the public health policy subsystem (Vize, 2020). It also pitted it against bodies such as WHO, which had concluded that e-cigarettes were far from safe. The issue here was not the question of whether vaping was less harmful than smoking, which it is. Rather the question was whether vaping itself created a market for new users that could then be targeted the producers to entice the young in particular into smoking. If decision makers only focused on the dose–response relationship between the chemicals in vaping and health, then they would neglect the broader evidence about behavioural change, most particularly by the manufacturers of vapes.

Particular problems of evidence arise when dealing with health care emergencies, where uncertain and conflicting evidence may need to be appraised rapidly as the basis of urgent decision-making. The difficulties that arise are well illustrated in the cases of COVID-19. One of the most challenging aspects of COVID-19 from the point of view of its control is asymptomatic transmission. In the early days of the pandemic, the possibility of asymptomatic transmission was not fully appreciated. At its meeting on 13 January 2020, the New and Emerging Respiratory Virus Threats Advisory Group (NERVTAG) took the view that the virus did not appear to be very transmissible, let alone asymptomatically transmissible (England and Wales High Court, 2022: paragraph 30). Others involved in giving scientific advice were sceptical about testing asymptomatic adults. On 28 January 2020, for example, the Scientific Advisory Group for Emergencies (SAGE) advised against testing asymptomatic individuals because of the possibility of false negatives. So, a correct understanding of the policy problem was not self-evident. Reliable policy-relevant understanding necessarily emerges from a community of agents operating in the domain of policy decision-making.

It can be argued that it is easy to overstate the difficulties of the science dealing with public health problems. One of the concerns here is that there is a long history of vested economic interests seizing on relatively minor uncertainties and scientific controversies to suggest that public health measures are unwarranted. Certainly, it may be hard to establish whether there are health harms arising from low levels of exposure to pollutants. However, there are many examples where health risks are so well established that vigorous public action is implied, including tobacco, excessive alcohol consumption, obesity, water pollution and air pollution.

In summary, although the principle of scientific integrity is at the core of public health policy, the science involved is what might be called 'policy science': that is to say, systematic understanding in the service of decision making. Practical science is more than applied science, since scientists applying their theories to the understanding of cause and effect relations may be free to adopt an agnostic attitude until further evidence becomes available. That freedom is not available to those who are applying their science for the determination of policy, when a policy choice is needed urgently.

Independence of policy advice

The framework document for UKHSA speaks about its balancing 'the needs for public health expertise, operational delivery, scientific integrity, independence in the delivery of policy advice and the necessary level of ministerial oversight and accountability to command public confidence' (DHSC, 2022a: paragraph 1.7, p 6). Built into the remit, therefore, is this balancing requirement. Policy advice should be independent but is to be balanced by accountability to ministers. The significance of this is that an executive agency is one stop short of being a fully independent body established by government, like the National Institute for Health and Care Excellence (NICE) or the Office for Budget Responsibility (OBR), both of which take full responsibility for the content of their publications and other pronouncements. Their status means that they can provide independent evidence for the public debate about policy. By contrast, an executive agency is subject to ministerial oversight and its autonomy from day-to-day departmental control is a way of giving it freedom to pursue government goals. Like UKHSA, PHE was an executive agency and was criticised for its lack of independence from government, restricting its ability to 'speak truth to power'.

Given UKHSA enjoys the same status, it remains unclear how it intends to avoid a similar fate. The problem is a deep-seated and pervasive one within government, with speaking truth to power being the exception not the rule.

It can be argued that there is a trade-off between independence and influence and that there are advantages in being close to government. Those who are optimistic about OHID hope that, as it is housed in the DHSC, its closeness to government will allow it to exercise greater influence and have a closer collaboration with ministers. Equally, however, there is a risk that OHID may disappear into Whitehall and become invisible, lacking even the limited degree of independence PHE had. To succeed, OHID has to be visible and have allies inside government, including the Chief Medical Officer for England, who also need to be visible.

Perhaps if UKHSA and also OHID had been established as arm's-length bodies they would have had greater independence from government and freedom to speak out. Indeed, such a status was enjoyed by the former Health Protection Agency which was folded into PHE when it was established.

One advantage of independence like that of NICE or the OBR is that it places an onus on government to explain why its decisions do not conform to the advice. Consider the case of alcohol control. Suppose a fully independent public health body were to favour policies of more stringent regulation (for example, restricting the number of licensed premises in an area), higher taxation or minimum unit pricing as being the most effective way to reduce the health risks of alcohol. Suppose, however, that these sorts of policies are opposed by those who hold to a libertarian ideology and who think that the state should not have a role in limiting the freedom of individuals 'to go to hell in their own way'. (See the next chapter for a fuller discussion of these arguments.) Should the public health body be required, as part of its accountability, to explain why it rejects these libertarian principles?

In answer to this question, we think not. We should think of the public health body as being delegated with the responsibility to explain to government what it regards as most effective in promoting the health of the public. It does not have the responsibility to engage in the ideological controversies that surround such policies. That is properly a political responsibility. The ability to speak truth to power implies an obligation on elected officials to be open to advice to which they personally or their political party may have ideological objections. Openness means ensuring that the advice is published rather than suppressed, so that the public can understand what the issues are. Public confidence will not be fostered if it is thought that elected officials are simply closing their minds to the advice that is being proffered.

This is an important aspect of the political leadership that is needed in the field of public health. Within the constitutional conventions of the UK, ministers should bear the ultimate responsibility for acting on or rejecting the advice that they are offered by any public health body modelled on the OBR. However, this should be done in public, not in private, and the OBR precedent could be adapted to health, as suggested by Lincoln and Lodge (2018). Thus, there would be an obligation on ministers to explain to parliament or a parliamentary committee why advice that was given was not accepted, and why the government judged the consequences of its own policy choices to be better than those suggested by the public health body. This would not, of course, completely control any arbitrary power to whom truth has to be spoken, but it would help tame that power and hold the government to account.

Political leadership, resources and intersectoral collaboration

The responsibilities of political leadership are also central to issues of resources and intersectoral collaboration. The ostensible reason for the demise of PHE was its inability to scale up its testing and tracing operation. However, as Sir Chris Whitty and Sir Patrick Vallance explained to the Covid-19 Inquiry (Booth, 2023), the failure lay not in the ability to test a relatively small number of cases but in the lack of resources to scale up the testing operation. Whitty explained clearly what were the implications of this failure for political responsibility, saying maintaining capacity between pandemics required investment and politicians would need to choose 'between having an insurance against future events and, for example, investing in pressures in the NHS during winter. That is a choice, and I think it has to be made explicit'. As UKHSA absorbs Test and Trace, there will be increasing pressure on its budget in the hope that resources can be released for other public sector policy areas. The test of political responsibility will be to insist that spending for contingency preparation, whether that be for extreme weather events or the outbreak of a major epidemic, should be protected in a way that was not true for PHE.

One problem for PHE, as we saw in Chapter 2, was the difficulty it has in coordinating action across central government departments, and both UKHSA and OHID are confronted with the same problem. Public health comprises numerous 'wicked problems' made up of public policy challenges that are 'complex, hard to resolve, keep shifting, have multiple causes and solutions, and cut across jurisdictions' (Hunter et al, 2022). Confronting them will be especially challenging in a government which, for all its rhetoric about 'levelling up', is topic- and department-focused rather than concerned with cross-government issues. Much will depend on the success of a new cross-government ministerial board for prevention. However, experience from previous arrangements of a similar nature does not offer much hope. OHID therefore has a steep hill to climb if it wants to lead a transformational agenda across the wider determinants of health, which demands a whole-of-government approach. The hill just got steeper following government delays in tackling child obesity and its failure to implement a national food strategy. Instead, and in keeping with the prevailing political ethos, there is a renewed focus on individual behaviour change and lifestyle choices rather than tackling the influence on health of commercial interests via taxation and regulation. If significant inroads into the population health agenda are to be made, then confronting powerful vested interests in, and lobbying from, the food and drinks industry and their 'friends' in government engaged in what has been termed 'institutional corruption' (Hunter et al, 2022: 799) cannot be avoided. Whether OHID has either the backing from government or competences for such a struggle remains doubtful in the extreme.

A further issue for PHE identified in Chapter 2 was the variable quality of its relationship to local government. The issue became particularly acute in England during the COVID-19 pandemic with the difficulties of test and trace. The successful tracing of contacts requires local knowledge. So if successful science, primarily a central responsibility, is to be translated into successful implementation of activity at the local level, then national government has to work with local government. The union of scientific strength and local operational capacity requires organisations at these different levels to be able to work well together. Like PHE, UKHSA is also organisationally separate from local authorities, so the question arises as to how far the liaison problems are likely to persist.

The new element in the equation is the creation of integrated care systems (ICSs), which bring together local authorities with NHS bodies, with the aim of taking a population perspective. In principle, their creation should work against the bias to the urgent, given their intended focus on population health. Yet, finding the space, and ensuring the skills and resources are in place, to go upstream while working in partnership with others across and at all levels of government is likely to prove tricky, especially at a time when the NHS is under great stress. The overall aim is to ensure joined-up care for patients in the localities for which they are responsible and to strengthen the health of the population in those places. It is still early in the evolution of ICSs to make a judgement on their likely success, but they do at least offer the best chance so far in the NHS's 75 years to do things differently, provided a context is created in which they can, as Hewitt states, 'thrive and deliver' (Hewitt, 2023: paragraph 1.23, p 15).

Notwithstanding this, however, the Conservative government's response to the recommendations of the Hewitt Review is not promising. Hewitt recommended the government convene a 'national mission for health improvement' that shifts the focus away from treating illness to promoting health and wellbeing. She suggests this could be led 'personally by the prime minister'. Her report also proposed that the share of local NHS budgets being spent on 'prevention' should be increased by at least one percentage point over the next five years. In response to these recommendations, the former proposal was deemed unnecessary by the government as 'we have already committed to a UK-wide Levelling Up health mission to narrow the gap in healthy life expectancy' and have 'established the Health Mission Working Group to provide a forum for working with other departments to explore opportunities for cross-government action to drive progress on the health mission'. The latter proposal is dismissed out of hand, with the government declaring: 'We do not agree with imposing a national expectation of an essentially arbitrary shift in spending' (DHSC, 2023). In short, we believe in business as usual.

Implementing the transformation

Transforming health systems is a complex, messy business with no quick or simple solutions (Hunter and Bengoa, 2023). The reforms underway in many countries across the world, including the UK, share a number of common features: a shift to integrated care reflecting demographic changes and the growth of multimorbidities; a renewed focus on population health to tackle rising health inequalities and the growing disease burden from non-communicable diseases; patient empowerment and community engagement; IT and digital health; knowledge management; and value-based payment methods. Overall, the intention is to move to a system centred on optimising health and well-being, and away from one dominated by ill health and care, much of which is provided in hospitals.

Change in complex health systems does not evolve in a sequential, linear fashion. Nor is it even inevitable. Health systems continually metamorphose in response to various pressures, including rapidly changing epidemiology, policy jolts (an extreme example being the impact of COVID-19, with implications for health systems that remain to be fully realised), to scientific and technological breakthroughs, and to disruptive innovations that are altering medical practice. Many of these developments were already underway prior to the pandemic but what it has done is to hasten their uptake and absorption into daily practice. Changes that might have taken five to ten years to enter into routine practice have become the new normal within a few weeks in many countries. However, had countries been more advanced in having in place a proactive, integrated and preventive population-based health system, the COVID-19 crisis might have been better, and more quickly, controlled.

Despite there being widespread agreement over why large-scale transformation is needed, when it comes to putting it into practice and ensuring that the changes are implemented in a joined-up, coherent and sustainable way, there is far less certainty about how to effect change of the type sought or to understand the factors that might impede it. This remains the case even where there exists sound evidence to underpin the desired changes.

While a policy implementation gap is nothing new, the policy context has become considerably more complex as the 'wicked problems' to which there are no simple or single solutions have come to dominate the agenda (Grint, 2008; Rittel and Webber, 1973). Such problems have been identified as 'adaptive challenges' (Heifetz et al, 2009). All too often policy failure is the result. Four broad contributors to policy failure may be identified: overly optimistic expectations; implementation in dispersed governance; inadequate collaborative policy making; and the vagaries of the political cycle (Hudson et al, 2019).

For a WHO health system transformation project (co-led by one of us – Hunter), a conceptual framework was chosen derived from research examining the reform of the NHS in the early 1990s (WHO, 2016 and 2018). The framework built on a receptive context for change framework developed by Pettigrew and colleagues (Pettigrew et al, 1992). Other frameworks, notably Kotter's eight steps for successful change (Kotter, 1995) and Kingdon's multiple streams approach (Kingdon, 1995), were included and cited to provide reinforcement and refinement to the insights offered by the receptive context for change framework.

For the WHO project, five factors were selected from the receptive context for change framework: environmental pressure; quality and coherence of policy; key people leading change; supportive organisational culture; and health professions, including managerial–clinical relations. These five factors can guide, shape and influence where and how transformational change occurs, but they are not items on a shopping list that can be chosen, or not at random. The factors are interrelated and must be aligned. If they push and pull in different directions, which is all too often the case in practice, efforts to achieve change are likely to fail. Conversely, even if all the factors are properly aligned, success is not guaranteed – there is 'no simple recipe or quick fix in managing complex change' (Pettigrew et al, 1992).

Building on these five factors are two additional issues that merit attention. First is establishing a sense of urgency so that the need for change cannot be ignored or deferred indefinitely. This emphasis on urgency also underlies the notion of the 'burning platform' as a trigger for change. Such a platform must surely be the impact of COVID-19 and the need to take public health seriously and invest in it with the NHS being seen as a key partner.

The second issue to attend to involves enabling 'quick wins' in order to demonstrate that the changes sought are having a positive and immediate impact even if embedding them in practice at pace and scale will take considerably longer. Securing quick wins is especially important in a context where the focus is on the short term at the expense of the long term. They provide reassurance to policy makers who may be under attack over their policies, and enable them to produce interim evidence that the changes can succeed and are working.

If the NHS is truly to evolve into a health system, then significant change is required in how it is positioned within the wider health system. Working alongside local authorities and other bodies, it needs to add its considerable weight to efforts to improve population health and reduce health inequalities. As a major employer across the country, it has a central role to play in the levelling up agenda. But for this shift to occur in the way the NHS operates and conceives of its mission, attention is needed to those factors that will enable change to succeed. We do not need more descriptions of the problem but documented examples of how change has occurred and policy has been made to stick, thereby helping to close the know–do gap.

We also need a new social contract to underpin these changes, an issue that we explore in the next chapter.

FIVE

A new social contract for public health

We have argued that there is a fundamental puzzle at the heart of the public health crisis that now faces the UK. Although the problems are large, there are many policy measures capable of addressing them that are highly cost-effective and for which there is robust evidence. The importance of these measures has been recognised for decades by informed commentators on health services, the latest example of which has been the creation of integrated care systems (ICSs) and the proposals from the Hewitt Review for government to give a lead in prioritising preventive measures. Unless government implements these measures, the burdens on the NHS will increase, forcing an increasing rationing of medical care among the sick. To be sure, the administrative and governance barriers to action can be formidable. The measures require interorganisational collaboration, never easy for any organisation let alone governments, and an ability at the heart of government to think long-term. The measures also require being explicit about the trade-offs, including the trade-off between more private consumer spending and greater public health protection, that are involved in making health truly public. They require addressing the commercial determinants of health, strengthening and supporting those commercial activities that promote health and regulating and disincentivising those commercial activities that harm health. In short, the challenges of public health require a relentless focus on implementation and policy learning, with firm political leadership to ensure that measures are put into practice and the organisational barriers to public policy coordination overcome.

In this context, the focus on finding one right organisational structure displayed in the abolition of Public Health England (PHE) is inadequate. The view, expressed by Matt Hancock as Secretary of State, that the creation of the UK Health Security Agency (UKHSA) in place of PHE would be sufficient to avoid a repeat of the failures to upscale testing and tracing on the part of PHE was an example of naive 'if only' thinking, resting on the assumption that if only PHE had been like the Robert Koch Institute all would be well. Yet distinguished witnesses to the Covid-19 Inquiry, like Sir Chris Whitty and Sir Patrick Vallance, suggested the failures of PHE were the results of successive public underfunding, such that the UK was left without adequate stocks of personal protective equipment or the facilities to manufacture vaccines. Without a reversal of such policies, UKHSA will have been set up to fail when the next pandemic occurs. Moreover, UKHSA itself will need to do a better job than PHE in forming constructive relations with public health departments in local authorities. Whether the separation of health protection and health promotion as part of the Hancock reforms makes sense, only time will tell. Much depends on how well UKHSA and the Office for Health Improvement and Disparities (OHID) can cooperate. Our own view is that the separation will make the task of improving public health more difficult, and that in choosing to be an outlier against the organisational patterns of Scotland, Wales and Northern Ireland, policy makers for England have made a mistake. Beyond these organisational questions, however, there are larger issues.

Public health policies use the instruments of political authority to promote the health of the population. Examining how that authority has been used in the UK over the last decade or so does not suggest a pattern of state overreach, as some critics of public health policies maintain, but of state underreach, involving a failure to take up and use policies and policy instruments that are known to be beneficial and effective. Such underreach is, of course, the result of over a decade of declining funding that has gone towards public health since 2010. More fundamentally, however, it is the result of a currently dominant public philosophy that typically underplays the importance of public health.

For much of the last 40 years, a significant element of that dominant public philosophy has been libertarianism, a form of what we have called 'vulgar individualism'. Libertarian objections to public health policies are often phrased as opposition to the 'nanny state'. According to this libertarian view, it is not a legitimate role for the state to promote the health of individuals. Rather, the health of individuals is a matter of personal responsibility. This is not a view confined to the margins of political activity. Under the Truss government, Thérèse Coffey, the Secretary of State for Health and Social Care, was known to be sceptical of public health measures, and she was not alone. On 14 September 2022 it was reported that Liz Truss, then prime minister, had launched a review of England's anti-obesity strategy as part of a wider deregulation initiative (BBC News, 2022). Even though the life of the Truss government was cut mercifully short, the scepticism it exhibited is an expression of a libertarian political philosophy in which it is said that governments have no proper role to play in supporting, encouraging or incentivising individuals to be healthy. It is a philosophy according to which that government is best which governs least.

So influential is this libertarian public philosophy that it is important to highlight the deficiencies of its vulgar individualism. However, this critical task is the prologue to a more positive account of legitimate state activity in relation to public health. In place of the ideals of the libertarian state, we propose a new social contract for public health incorporating the principles of what we shall call 'social individualism', a commitment to properly using the instruments of collective political authority to create the conditions for individual choice and fulfilment.

Why libertarianism fails

As the Nuffield Council on Bioethics (2007) pointed out in its report on public health, those who are sceptical of public health often invoke a principle of individual liberty that was expressed by John Stuart Mill in his statement of the so called harm principle:

> [T]he sole end for which mankind are warranted, individually or collectively, in interfering with the liberty of action of any of their number, is self-protection. That the only purpose for which power can be rightfully exercised over any member of a civilized community, against his will, is to prevent harm to others. His own good, either physical or moral, is not sufficient warrant. He cannot rightfully be compelled to do or forbear because it will be better for him to do so, because it will make him happier, because, in the opinion of others, to do so would be wise, or even right. (Mill, 1859: 14)

This quotation contains two principles. The first says that it can sometimes be a reason for collective interference with the freedom of individuals that such interference will prevent harm to others. (Mill did not think that causing harm was always a reason to interfere, since the harm of the interference might outweigh the harm prevented.) The second principle says that promoting their own good is never a reason to interfere with the freedom of individuals. It is this second anti-paternalist principle that libertarians typically invoke in their opposition to public health measures. That some individuals would be healthier if they were interfered with – say, to help them stop smoking, reduce their alcohol intake or lose weight – is not a legitimate use of state authority. As Mill put it, their own good, either physical or moral, is not sufficient warrant.

But are things quite so simple? Even when Mill allows that harm to others is a valid possible ground for interference, it is unclear how widely that principle is to be understood. For example, it is not clear how far the risk of causing harm to others would license interference. Even taken on its own terms, Mill's argument is more subtle that some of his contemporary libertarian admirers allow, accepting, for example, that some compulsion might be needed to provide public goods for a society – for example, giving evidence in court or bearing one's fair share of the common defence (Mill, 1859: 108–09). Moreover, Mill was writing long before there was a scientific understanding of the causes of ill health and long before improved nutrition, sanitary reforms and vaccination had shown their capacity to reduce disease and improve population health. He also wrote long before the creation of collectively organised health care systems, whether based on taxation or social insurance. If the growth of public health science highlights the capacity to promote population health, the existence of a collectively funded health care system provides a reason for including public health measures as instruments of public policy.

Consider the case of obesity. Obesity is a major cause of ill health, notably diabetes, the effects of which increase demands on the limited resources of the NHS, with type 2 diabetes on some estimates absorbing some ten per cent of total expenditure. The causes of the growth of obesity across many societies are much debated, with changes in the occupational structure leading to more sedentary jobs, travel patterns making for less exercise, changes in the production of food, and the increased consumption of high energy foods all being implicated. The solutions offered to tackle such a complex issue are also much debated (Metcalfe and Sasse, 2023). In general, politicians are reluctant to resort to 'nanny state' measures if these can be avoided, and obesity provides a good example of the conflicts and tensions evident in devising a coherent policy response and where the focus should lie. In the case of the current government, there is considerable appeal in using weight-loss drugs in place of other measures to encourage healthier lifestyles or going upstream to tackle the commercial determinants of health. But this risks promoting measures which support the pharmaceutical industry, with implications for society that remain to be fully determined. An obesity strategy reliant on weight-loss drugs would mean many people depending on them, possibly for life, with numerous side effects to contend with, in addition to the cost of such a policy (McCartney, 2023).

In this complex mixture of influencing causes and possible solutions it is all but impossible to factor out what is a matter of personal choice and willpower, and what is a matter of the patterns of social life in which people participate. Moreover, policies aimed at modifying the social causes that bring about obesity will in any case have to be targeted at individuals. However, suppose for the sake of argument that it were possible to identify those elements of obesity that were the product of individual choice and for which individuals could be held rightly responsible. Would it follow that there was no reason to interfere with those free choices? Interestingly, one leading libertarian thinker, Hayek, thought not. In *The Constitution of Liberty* Hayek not only assigns a substantial role to national institutions to assure income support in old age, unemployment or sickness, he takes it as 'an obvious corollary' of the state's role that it is right to compel individuals to insure or otherwise provide against the common hazards of life because 'by neglecting to make such provision, they would become a charge to the public' (Hayek, 1960: 285–6). Thus, individuals should be compelled to pay into schemes of social assistance.

Should you then think that how individuals incur risks in their life is a matter that is purely up to them, you face Hayek's objection. The members of society will not simply stand by and let the youthful rake become the suffering old wretch. They will feel compelled to provide at least minimal assistance.

So it is with obesity and illness. The NHS will not turn away from its doors those who are suffering type 2 diabetes, even if it were clear that those suffering the disease brought it on themselves. As a result, the price for being unconditionally libertarian is borne by the general taxpayer. In such a system, citizens may feel that their own financial self-protection would permit some health promotion measures, all of which are mild and nowhere near strict prohibition, in order to reduce overall costs. There are many other reasons why a responsible government will reasonably want to push ahead with public health measures, even if it were to fall foul of respecting Mill's harm principle. But even libertarians ought to be conscious that the 'nanny state' is one aspect of the fiscally responsible state.

More fundamentally, there is a neglect by libertarians of the positive role the state can play in promoting health and well-being, despite libertarians themselves being beneficiaries of state action. Individualist libertarians buy products that are tested for safety, so that their furniture is not a fire hazard or the toys their children play with do not contain sharp objects that can be poked in the children's eyes. The same children are protected from contracting infectious diseases by organised vaccination programmes, or from exposure to health harms by restrictions on the advertising of products with health risks. Adult libertarians are protected from the spread of infectious diseases, for example, Ebola, brought into the country by visitors. They consume foodstuffs that are regulated for their conditions of production and the purity of their ingredients, and in the case of some products, like bread, fortified by folic acid and iron, or, in the case of soft drinks, manufactured with reduced sugar content. They drink from tap water that is tested for its purity and safety. They can take advantage of well-organised screening programmes for the early detection of cancers. They benefit from the emergency preparedness of the medical facilities when there is extreme weather. When their gas or electricity is serviced, it is done by qualified and certified personnel, so that operational safety is maintained. They travel in vehicles required to undergo compulsory annual safety checks, with restrictions on those that can drive, with all legally required to have third-party insurance. Public roads have been increasingly well engineered by the authorities so that road accidents and deaths have fallen consistently over the decades. Street lighting is provided by the highways authorities.

Libertarians enjoy all of these benefits while decrying the 'nanny state' and the 'red tape' of regulation. In fact, they would enjoy more benefits were air pollution more stringently controlled or bathing waters more effectively protected from sewage discharges or were alcohol controls more vigorously pursued to prevent town and city centres being no-go areas for many on Friday and Saturday nights. Libertarians decry the 'nanny state' because for them the market is not just a good servant but the master to which they are in thrall.

At the root of the shortcomings of libertarianism is the fallacy of vulgar individualism: the view that the interests of individuals are best served when the state is organised on the principle that that government is best which governs least. In place of vulgar individualism we need a social individualism, which identifies the collective conditions for individual choice and fulfilment. To escape the thraldom of libertarianism, we need a new social contract.

The social contract for public health

A social contract states the charter of the rights and responsibilities in which the members of a society participate, as well as the principled basis for its public policies. It offers a definition of those actions that must be addressed collectively. Protection from transmissible diseases, control of environmental pollution or preparing public services for emergency events are not activities that individuals on their own can will into existence. In many cases they deal with spillover effects from others in relation to which a multitude of individuals are vulnerable. In consequence, they need to be organised collectively as public services if they are to be effective. What, then, are the elements of the new social contract that is needed for public health?

In the first place, it would have a focus on prevention. As we have noted, there is good evidence that a wide range of public health measures would prevent more serious conditions developing and reduce demand on the NHS. However, it is not enough to state the abstract advantages of prevention. That giving priority to prevention would translate into more health gain than putting ever increasing amounts of money into the NHS may be true, but it is hard for a government to act on since the gains secured by public health are in the future and impossible to identify with any one set of patients. The electoral and other incentives to deal with the problem of hospital waiting lists or access to GPs are considerable, by comparison with the future benefit to hypothetical unknown people. Political leadership is needed to confront this problem, paying attention to priorities and the sequencing of a heterogeneous range of measures.

Secondly, the new social contract requires a precautionary state, paying attention not only to known imminent hazards but also to remote and uncertain ones. This is a hard lesson to learn for those who live in a society in which 'just in time' has become the norm. Of course we benefit from supermarket shelves that are filled with fresh goods delivered on a just-in-time basis or distribution systems that can deliver to your door the following morning an order that you made this evening. But we mistake the marginal benefit to us each as individuals for the structural benefit of collective protection if we suppose that public health can be supplied on a just-in-time basis and that, provided we have the resources in reserve, we can scale up activity at will.

The experience of COVID-19 illustrates the failure of just-in-time thinking and a neglect of precaution. Despite the precedent of SARS, the planning for the anticipated pandemic was based on the assumption that it would take the form of a serious flu, rather than having the asymptomatic transmission possibilities that COVID-19 had. However, precaution is at the core of health protection, not only in relation to infectious diseases but also in relation to environmental hazards like air pollution. Precaution means being alert to possible hazards even when the understanding of their effects is uncertain or contested. This does not mean giving credence to purely speculative hypotheses, but it does mean horizon-scanning for likely possibilities that have hitherto been neglected.

The philosophy of social individualism that requires prevention and precaution also requires social solidarity in the face of health inequalities. Social individualism recognises that policies for the most vulnerable are not policies for a particular group in society, but policies for all of us when we are in need. Nothing is more obvious than that we are born vulnerable and utterly dependent, grow into independence if we are lucky, usually acquiring responsibilities to those younger than us, before, unless we are very fortunate in avoiding the scourges of old age, facing another period of dependence. What we need from public policies is the support to resilience over the life cycle. In this enterprise, each one of us must be both giver and receiver.

The vocabulary of 'levelling up' obscures these basic truths. It portrays a world in which one group of people – the left behind – are helped by another group of people – the affluent – to the advantage of the former and the detriment of the latter. But things are not so simple. The well-off pensioner forced to wait for hours for emergency treatment after a fall, the young professional couple who find that one of them is working solely to pay for childcare, or the business that cannot find trained technical staff all suffer from the lack of public support that a well-functioning social contract would provide, including adequate provision for health and social care, affordable childcare and high-quality education and training. The lustre of private affluence loses its shine amid public penury.

Beveridge's five giants of disease, want, squalor, ignorance and idleness may now take different forms, but they exist, and all too often they cluster with one another. Health inequalities are the product of social and economic patterns that link ill health with poverty, poor housing, lack of education and job insecurity. It follows that solidaristic policies to deal with those other giants will contribute to dealing with the giant of disease. This does not mean that to improve health requires solving all the problems of society. But it does mean that public health policies will be more effective when they are seen as an element in a more comprehensive programme.

The challenges facing the creation of a precautionary state – a state whose policies address the need to plan for the hazards that may come our collective way – are many, and there is, of course, no easy recipe. However, in rising to those challenges it will be necessary to address the short-termism that is too often a feature of democratic politics, the populist promise that we can have our cake and eat it. The costs of precaution, like all investment, come early and the benefits come later. When people are hard-pressed financially, it is hard to persuade them to give up something now for the promise of something in the future.

Even more difficult in the pursuit of the precautionary state is that the benefits are often those of security rather than something that is experienced directly. Like any form of insurance, the hope is that you do not have to call on the policy. If this is a sober lesson for us as individuals, it is an even harder lesson for us as a collective body. A populist politics that wishes away the need for planning and relies on facile slogans to attain office – 'the unbearable lightness of politics' as the historian, Tony Judt (2010) put it – undercuts the sobriety that is needed for government in the interest of the people.

Is social individualism a partisan political philosophy? In one sense, it obviously is. It is partisan in that it is committed to the collective organisation of society that makes public health possible. It is partisan for public health. However, this does not mean that it is partisan in a narrow party-political sense. In his great, and underappreciated, study of the ideological heritage of the British political tradition, Greenleaf (1983) identified the collectivist elements present in liberalism, conservatism and socialism. In the liberal tradition stand the names of T.H. Green and Keynes; in the socialist tradition the Webbs and Fabianism; and in the conservative tradition Disraeli, Neville Chamberlain and Macmillan. For all the differences among those in these different traditions, and indeed within those traditions, it is clear that none subscribed to the view that that government is best which governs least. All saw a role for an active state. In what, then, should the state be active if public health is to be promoted?

A manifesto

A crisis can easily induce a sense of despair at the scale of the challenges that it presents. But in the case of public health, despair should be shunned. Much that needs to be done is already understood and supported by a robust evidence base. Some measures could be adopted within the first hundred days of a new government. Others will take longer to implement and have effect, but they can be planned for now. The most constructive approach is to start with what can be done early in the life of a new government and over time, as further measures are added, develop the momentum for cumulative change. The Hewitt Review, the Faculty of Public Health and the Association of Directors of Public Health (ADPH) have offered a set of overlapping proposals that, taken together and implemented vigorously, would make for health being public.

A good place to start would be with the Hewitt Review and its plea for priority to be given to population health matched by new investment. If the creation of integrated care systems is to be justified, they will need a clear strategy to make public health measures a priority, and funds need to be made available within the NHS budget for work on prevention. In addition, there is a consensus that government needs to invest something like an additional £0.9bn in local public health budgets in England, with equivalent investments made in public health in the devolved nations. The ADPH has made clear the commitment of its members to work actively to make sure that new money is well spent in addressing the challenges: for example, by developing and implementing harm-reduction approaches to drug misuse.

Investment also needs to be made in the centralised health protection systems so that the UK does not suffer a repeat of its vulnerability to the COVID-19 pandemic when the next major transmissible disease comes along. More also needs to be done to address current risks like antibiotic resistance, and the climate emergency will require better understanding of how best to respond to, and mitigate the effects of, extreme weather events. Moreover, as the current concerns about vaping show, health protection agencies need to be alert to changes in behaviour that can set public health back years.

Some will question such spending priorities in an economic context in which resources will be badly strained. But there is a need to tap into the emerging consensus that health and wealth go together, with health being seen as an investment and not a cost or drag on economic growth. A focus on growth to the exclusion of investing in health has failed us badly, as the experience of COVID-19 and its aftermath have demonstrated. We cannot afford as a country to lose more people from the workforce as a result of illness.

A redirection of spending is also needed to address health inequalities, particularly those that arise through poverty. The government should introduce a dedicated health inequalities strategy and set clear targets for how this will be achieved. In particular, there urgently needs to be a budgetary commitment over a number of years to eliminate childhood poverty, through increasing child benefits, expanding early years provision of childcare and reintroducing the Sure Start programme. Such measures would not require new legislation, but a new Child Poverty Act which commits to ending child poverty in all parts of the UK by 2030 would solidify the commitment.

On obesity and food policy the starting point would be to implement the recommendations of the Dimbleby (2021) report, including a sugar and salt reformulation tax, and subsidies for healthier eating, including extending eligibility for free school meals. This could be done almost immediately by an incoming government. As part of that strategy, there needs to be a continuing programme of research and regulation on ultra-processed foods. Also, active travel ought to be thought of as an integral part of the anti-obesity strategy, and government needs to pursue more vigorously its currently stalled active travel policies, including infrastructure for cycling and walking.

On alcohol control, the example of Scotland needs to be followed, with the introduction of minimum unit pricing. This would encourage the development of low-alcohol drinks and would run with the tide of much lower rates of alcohol consumption among younger groups.

Urban air pollution brings longer-term challenges, involving as it does the installation of new technologies for energy and transport systems. Immediately, however, it is possible to expand low emission zones. Here again an active transport policy is central. The need to respond to the climate emergency is at one with the promotion of public health, as renewables replace the use of fossil fuels. There should also be an encouragement of green spaces and the planting of trees in urban areas, for their health as well as their environmental benefits, policies that WHO is proposing for the European Region.

As we have argued in this book, at the heart of public health policy is the need to work in a cross-organisational and cross-sectoral way. This will not happen without strong political leadership, but to embed a cross-government commitment to public health, new consolidated legislation is needed, not only to place a duty on all government departments to respect in their policies the claims of health protection and promotion, but also to place an obligation on government to account for the pursuit of its policies within the framework of explicit goals. Like financial probity, public health should not be compromised.

As this list, which is only partial, makes clear, the scale of the challenges facing the country goes far beyond the public health system in isolation. As we have emphasised throughout this book, unless our broken political and governance system, with its numerous systemic failings, is confronted, then attempts to tackle complex problems like public health, which requires long-term commitment, proper investment and a relentless focus on delivery, will fail.

The winds of change have been blowing through the country. COVID-19 has gravely affected everyone. How to respond to public health challenges is being actively debated in the UK Covid-19 Inquiry. The NHS is facing a crisis of performance and of staff morale with no real solutions in sight. Institutions that are not the usual commentators on health issues are viewing the importance of a healthy workforce as a prerequisite to any economic recovery. So now, more than at any time, there are considerable opportunities for action but only if government has the political will and competence to act. A key opportunity will present itself over the next year or so – a general election. Whoever forms the next UK government cannot afford to ignore the challenges set out in this book. If the public's health is to become the priority that is urgently called for, the opportunity should be seized.

Appendix: note on original research study

The background to this book was a research study that took place in 2021 and 2022. It sought to understand the circumstances surrounding the abolition of the main institution responsible for public health in England – Public Health England (PHE) – and its replacement by the UK Health Security Agency and the Office for Health Improvement and Disparities. As well as collecting data from published reports, national and parliamentary committee meetings and interviews, we also collected information on the structure of public health governmental organisations in the UK. The main study findings can be found here: https://arc-sl.nihr.ac.uk/sites/defa ult/files/uploads/files/public-health-report-sept-2022-final. pdf (Littlejohns et al, 2022c).

The relevant issues that emerged as we described how PHE was closed can be found in a paper we published in *Health Economics Policy and Law* (Weale et al, 2023).

While the reasons were complex, they could be summarised by two competing interpretations: an 'official' explanation, which highlights the failure of PHE to scale up its testing capacity in the early weeks of the COVID-19 pandemic as the fundamental reason for closing it down; and a 'sceptical' interpretation, which ascribes the decision to blame-avoidance behaviour on the part of leading government figures. We reviewed crucial claims in these two competing explanations, exploring the arguments for and against each proposition. We concluded that neither was adequate and that the inability to address the problem of testing (which triggered the decision to close PHE) lies deeper, in the absence of the norms of responsible government in UK politics and the state. However, our findings did provide some guidance to the two new organisations established to replace PHE to maximise their impact on public health.

We then continued our thinking of what was required and presented a flavour of it in a *Lancet Public Health* Viewpoint article by Hunter, Littlejohns and Weale on 'Reforming the public health system in England' (Hunter et al, 2022).

We came to the conclusion that a completely new way of thinking about public health was required, and that would only be achieved by establishing a new social contract with the British people.

Other publications from the original research project include:

- Blog post: 'Gone and even forgotten ... what did Public Health England do (or not do) to deserve this?', NIHR ARC South London, 23 March 2022 (Littlejohns et al, 2022a).
- Blog post: 'Evidence – was it really used in the Covid-19 pandemic? A key issue for the Covid-19 inquiry to address', NIHR ARC South London, 22 April 2022 (Kelly et al, 2022).
- Blog post: '"Bonfire of the Quangos" – let's make a pyre of this perennial ritual', NIHR ARC South London, 24 May 2022 (Littlejohns et al, 2022b).
- Blog post: 'Designing public health governance: its challenges, consequences and key lessons for the Covid-19 Public Inquiry', NIHR ARC South London, 28 June 2022 (Johnson et al, 2022).

References

Acheson, E.D. (1988) 'On the state of the public health [The fourth Duncan lecture]', *Public Health*, 102(5): 431–7.

Alexiou, A., Fahy, K., Mason, K., Bennett, D., Brown, H., Bambra, C., et al (2021) 'Local government funding and life expectancy in England: A longitudinal study', *Lancet Public Health*, 6(9): e641–7.

Anderson, H. (2023) 'Hunt wanted 50pc cut to public health, says ex-PHE boss', *Health Service Journal*, [online] 28 June, available from: https://www.hsj.co.uk/finance-and-efficiency/hunt-wan ted-50pc-cut-to-public-health-says-ex-phe-boss/7035077.article

Atkinson, R.W., Carey, I.M., Kent, A.J., van Staa, T.P., Anderson, H.R. and Cook, D.G. (2013) 'Long-term exposure to outdoor air pollution and incidence of cardiovascular diseases', *Epidemiology*, 24(1): 44–53.

Bambra, C. and Marmot, M. (2023) 'Expert report for the UK Covid-19 Public Inquiry, Module 1: Health Inequalities', [online] 30 May, available from: https://covid19.public-inquiry.uk/ documents/inq000195843-expert-report-by-professor-clare-bam bra-and-professor-sir-michael-marmot-dated--30-may-2023/

Bambra, C., Munford, L., Alexandros, A., Barr, B., Brown, H., Davies, H., et al (2020) 'COVID-19 and the Northern Powerhouse: Tackling inequalities for UK health and productivity', Newcastle: Northern Health Science Alliance.

BBC News. (2022) 'Anti-obesity strategy to be reviewed due to cost-of-living crisis', BBC News, [online] 14 September, available from: https://www.bbc.co.uk/news/uk-politics-62900076

Birkland, T.A. (1998) 'Focusing events, mobilization, and agenda setting', *Journal of Public Policy*, 18(1): 53–74.

Booth, R. (2023) 'Chris Whitty: UK should have focused more on stopping Covid-type pandemic', The Guardian, [online] 22 June, available from: https://www.theguardian.com/uk-news/2023/jun/22/chris-whitty-uk-should-have-focused-more-on-stopping-covid-type-pandemic

Boswell, J., Cairney, P. and St Denny, E. (2019) 'The politics of institutionalizing preventive health', *Social Science & Medicine*, 228: 202–10. https://doi.org/10.1016/j.socscimed.2019.02.051

Buck, D. (2020) 'The English local government public health reforms: An independent assessment', The King's Fund, [online] available from: https://www.kingsfund.org.uk/sites/default/files/2020-01/LGA%20PH%20reforms%20-%20final.pdf

Cambiano, V., Miners, A. and Phillips, A. (2016) 'What do we know about the cost-effectiveness of HIV preexposure prophylaxis, and is it affordable?', *Current Opinion in HIV and AIDS*, 11(1): 56–66.

Chief Medical Officer's Report (2022) 'Chief Medical Officer's annual report 2022: Air pollution', London: Department of Health and Social Care, [online] 8 December, available from: https://www.gov.uk/government/publications/chief-medical-officers-annual-report-2022-air-pollution

Clark, P. (2020) '"Problems of today and tomorrow": Prevention and the National Health Service in the 1970s', *Social History of Medicine*, 33(3): 981–1000.

Connolly, A.M. and PHE. (2016) 'National action on health inequalities: The NHS and the new public health system', [online] 12 May, available from: https://www.kingsfund.org.uk/sites/default/files/media/Annmarie_Connolly_PDF.pdf

Department of Health. (2010) 'Healthy lives, healthy people: Our strategy for public health in England', London: The Stationery Office, GOV.UK, [online] 30 November, available from: https://assets.publishing.service.gov.uk/government/uploads/system/uploads/attachment_data/file/216096/dh_127424.pdf

Department of Health. (2016) 'Government response to the House of Commons Health Committee Report on Public Health Post-2013 (Second Report of Session 2016–17)', London: The Stationery Office, GOV.UK, [online] available from: https://assets.publishing.service.gov.uk/government/uploads/system/uploads/attachment_data/file/573529/Gov_Reponse_Cm_9378_web.pdf

Department of Health and Social Care. (2022a) 'Framework Document between the Department of Health and Social Care and the UK Health Security Agency', GOV.UK, [online] 27 January, available from: https://data.parliament.uk/DepositedPapers/Files/DEP2022-0169/Framework_Document_between_DHSC_and_UKSHA.pdf

Department of Health and Social Care. (2022b) 'Letter from Maggie Throup to Professor Dame Jenny Harries, UKHSA chief executive', GOV.UK, [online] 12 August, available from: https://www.gov.uk/government/publications/ukhsa-priorities-in-2022-to-2023/letter-from-maggie-throup-to-professor-dame-jenny-harries-ukhsa-chief-executive

Department of Health and Social Care. (2023) 'Government response to the House of Commons Health and Social Care Committee's seventh report of session 2022 to 2023 on "Integrated care systems: autonomy and accountability"', [online] 14 June, available from: https://www.gov.uk/government/publications/government-response-to-the-hscc-report-and-the-hewitt-review-on-integrated-care-systems/government-response-to-the-house-of-commons-health-and-social-care-committees-seventh-report-of-session-2022-to-2023-on-integrated-care-systems-aut

Department of Health and Social Security. (1976) *Prevention and Health: Everybody's Business*, London: HMSO.

Dimbleby, H. (2021) 'National Food Strategy: The plan', The National Food Strategy, [online] available from: https://www.nationalfoodstrategy.org/

England and Wales High Court. (2022) *R. (Gardner and Harris) v. Secretary of State for Health and Social Care* [2022] EWHC 967, British and Irish Legal Information Institute, [online] 27 April, available from: https://www.bailii.org/ew/cases/EWHC/Admin/2022/967.html

Exworthy, M. and Hunter, D.J. (2011) 'The challenge of joined-up government in tackling health inequalities', *International Journal of Public Administration*, 34(4): 201–12. https://doi.org/10.1080/01900692.2011.551749

Faculty of Public Health. (2023) 'FPH policy briefings', Faculty of Public Health, [online], available from: https://www.fph.org.uk/policy-advocacy/what-we-think/fph-policy-briefs/

Friel, S., Collin, J., Daube, M., Depoux, A., Freudenberg, N., Gilmore, A.B., et al (2023) 'Commercial determinants of health: Future directions', *The Lancet*, 401(10383): 1229–40.

Gilmore, A.B., Fabbri, A., Baum, F., Bertscher, A., Bondy, K., Chang, H.-J., et al (2023) 'Defining and conceptualising the commercial determinants of health', *The Lancet*, 401(10383): 1194–231.

Gilmore, I., Bauld, L. and Britton, J. (2018) 'Public Health England's capture by the alcohol industry', *British Medical Journal*, 362: k3928.

Global Health Security Index. (2019) 'Global Health Security Index 2019: Building collective action and accountability', GHS Index, [online] available from: https://www.ghsindex.org/wp-content/uploads/2019/10/2019-Global-Health-Security-Index.pdf

Greenleaf, W.H. (1983) *The British Political Tradition, Volume 2: The Ideological Heritage*, London: Routledge.

Greer, S.L. (2008) 'Devolution and divergence in UK health policies', *British Medical Journal*, 337: a2616.

Greer, S.L. (2016) 'Devolution and health in the UK: Policy and its lessons since 1998', *British Medical Bulletin*, 118(1): 16–24. https://doi.org/10.1093/bmb/ldw013

Griffiths, S., Jewell, T. and Donnelly, P. (2005) 'Public health in practice: The three domains of public health', *Public Health*, 119(10): 907–13.

Grint, K. (2008) 'Wicked problems and clumsy solutions: The role of leadership', *Clinical Leader*, 1(2): 54–68.

Hayek, F.A. (1960) *The Constitution of Liberty*, London: Routledge & Kegan Paul.

Heifetz, R.A., Grashow, A. and Linsky, M. (2009) *The Practice of Adaptive Leadership: Tools and Tactics for Changing Your Organisation and the World*, Boston: Harvard Business Publishing

Hewitt, P. (2023) 'The Hewitt Review: An independent review of integrated care systems', GOV.UK, [online] 4 April, available from: https://assets.publishing.service.gov.uk/government/uplo ads/system/uploads/attachment_data/file/1148568/the-hew itt-review.pdf

Horton, R. (2020) 'COVID-19 is not a pandemic', *The Lancet*, 396(10255): 874, https://doi.org/10.1016/S0140-6736(20)32000-6

House of Commons Public Accounts Committee. (2015) 'Public Health England's grant to local authorities: Forty-third report of session 2014–15', HC 893, London: The Stationery Office. [Online] 3 March, available from https://publications.parliament. uk/pa/cm201415/cmselect/cmpubacc/893/893.pdf

House of Commons Health Committee. (2014) 'Public Health England: Eighth report of session 2013–14', HC 840, London: The Stationery Office. [Online] 4 February, available from: https://publications.parliament.uk/pa/cm201314/cmsel ect/cmhealth/840/840.pdf

House of Commons Health Committee. (2016) 'Public health post-2013: Second report of session 2016–17', HC 140, GOV.UK, [online] 18 July, available from: https://publications.parliament. uk/pa/cm201617/cmselect/cmhealth/140/140.pdf

Hudson, B., Hunter, D. and Peckham, S. (2019) 'Policy failure and the policy-implementation gap: Can policy support programs help?', *Policy Design and Practice*, 2(1): 1–14. https://doi.org/ 10.1080/25741292.2018.1540378

Hunter, D.J. (2016) 'Public health: Unchained or shackled?', in M. Exworthy, R. Mannion and M. Powell (eds) *Dismantling the NHS? Evaluating the Impact of Health Reforms*, Bristol: Policy Press, pp 191–210.

Hunter, D.J. (2019) 'Looking forward to the next 70 years: From a National Ill-Health Service to a National Health System', *Health Economics, Policy and Law*, 14(1): 11–14. https://doi.org/10.1017/S1744133118000099

Hunter, D.J. and Bengoa, R. (2023) 'Meeting the challenge of health system transformation in European countries', *Policy and Society*, 42(1): 14–27. https://doi.org/10.1093/polsoc/puac022

Hunter, D.J., Littlejohns, P. and Weale, A. (2022) 'Reforming the public health system in England', *The Lancet Public Health*, 7(9): e797–800. https://doi.org/10.1016/S2468-2667(22)00199-2

Hunter, D.J., Marks, L. and Smith, K.E. (2010) *The Public Health System in England*, Bristol: Policy Press.

Iacobucci, G. (2020), 'Public Health England is axed in favour of new health protection agency', *British Medical Journal*, 370: m3257. https://www.bmj.com/content/370/bmj.m3257

IPPR Commission on Health and Prosperity. (2023) 'Healthy people, prosperous lives', Institute for Public Policy Research, [online] 27 April, available from: https://www.ippr.org/research/publications/healthy-people-prosperous-lives

Johnson, J., Littlejohns, P. and Weale, A. (2022) 'Designing public health governance: its challenges, consequences and key lessons for the Covid-19 Public Inquiry', NIHR ARC South London, [online] 28 June, available from: https://arc-sl.nihr.ac.uk/news-insights/blog-and-commentary/designing-public-health-governance-its-challenges-consequences

Judt, T. (2010) *Ill Fares the Land*, Harmondsworth: Penguin Books.

Kelly, M.P., Littlejohns, P. and Markham, S. (2022) 'Evidence – was it really used in the Covid-19 pandemic? A key issue for the Covid-19 inquiry to address', NIHR ARC South London, [online] 22 April, available from: https://arc-sl.nihr.ac.uk/news-insights/blog-and-commentary/evidence-was-it-really-used-covid-19-pandemic-key-issue-covid-19

Kickbusch, I., Allen, L. and Franz, C. (2016) 'The commercial determinants of health', *The Lancet Global Health*, 4(12): e895–6. https://doi.org/10.1016/S2214-109X(16)30217-0

Kinder, T. (2020) 'McKinsey earnt £560,000 for giving "vision" to new English pandemic body', *Financial Times*, [online] 19 August, available from: https://www.ft.com/content/3cc76ad4-4d75-4e07-9f6d-476611fbb28f

Kingdon, J.W. (1995) *Agendas, Alternatives, and Public Policies* (2nd edn), New York: Harper Collins.

Knai, C., Petticrew, M., Mays, N., Capewell, S., Cassidy, R., Cummins, S., et al (2018) 'Systems thinking as a framework for analyzing commercial determinants of health', *The Milbank Quarterly*, 96(3): 472–98.

Kotter, J.P. (1995) 'Leading change: Why transformation efforts fail', *Harvard Business Review*, [online] May–June, available from: https://hbr.org/1995/05/leading-change-why-transformation-efforts-fail-2

Lacy-Nichols, J., Nandi, S., Mialon, M., McCambridge, J., Lee, K., Jones, A., et al (2023) 'Conceptualising commercial entities in public health: Beyond unhealthy commodities and transnational corporations', *The Lancet*, 401(10383): 1214–28.

Lalonde, M. (1974) *A New Perspective on the Health of Canadians*, Ottawa: Health Canada.

Lancet Countdown. (2022) 'The Lancet Countdown', [online] available from: https://www.lancetcountdown.org/

Lewer, D. and Bibby, J. (2021) 'Cuts to local government funding and stalling life expectancy', *The Lancet Public Health*, [online] 12 July, available from: https://doi.org/10.1016/S2468-2667(21)00136-5

Lincoln, P. and Lodge, H. (2018) 'Can an Office of Budget Responsibility for Population Health improve fiscal and economic planning to improve the public's health and well-being?', UK Public Health Network, [online] September, available from: https://ukpublichealthnetwork.org.uk/wp/wp-content/uploads/2019/02/OBR-for-population-health-discussion-paper-final.pdf

Littlejohns, P., Khatun, T. and Hunter, D.J. (2022) 'Gone and even forgotten ... what did Public Health England do (or not do) to deserve this?', NIHR ARC South London, [online] 23 March, available from: https://arc-sl.nihr.ac.uk/news-insights/blog-and-commentary/gone-and-even-forgotten-what-did-public-health-england-do-or-not

Littlejohns, P., Khatun, T. and Hunter, D.J. (2022b) ' "Bonfire of the Quangos" – let's make a pyre of this perennial ritual', NIHR ARC South London, [online] 24 May, available from: https://arc-sl.nihr.ac.uk/news-insights/blog-and-commentary/bonfire-quangos-lets-make-pyre-perennial-ritual

Littlejohns, P., Khatun, T., Knight, A., Hunter, D.J., Markham, S., Coultas, C., et al (2022c) 'Lessons from the demise of Public Health England: Where next for UK public health?', NIHR ARC South London, [online] September, available from: https://arc-sl.nihr.ac.uk/sites/default/files/uploads/files/public-health-report-sept-2022-final.pdf

Marmot, M. (2020) 'Why did England have Europe's worst Covid figures? The answer starts with austerity', *The Guardian*, [online] 10 August, available from: https://www.theguardian.com/commentisfree/2020/aug/10/england-worst-covid-figures-austerity-inequality

Marmot, M. (2022) 'A return to austerity will further damage the public's health', *British Medical Journal*, 379: o2507. https://doi.org/10.1136/bmj.o2507

Marmot, M., Allen, J., Boyce, T., Goldblatt, P. and Morrison, J. (2020) 'Health equity in England: The Marmot Review 10 years on', London: Institute of Health Equity, The Health Foundation, [online] February, available from: https://www.health.org.uk/publications/reports/the-marmot-review-10-years-on

Marshall, C. (2020) 'Air pollution death ruling: What comes next?', BBC News, [online] 17 December, available from: https://www.bbc.co.uk/news/science-environment-55352247

Marshall, L., Clay, T. and Bibby, J. (2021) 'Health at the heart of recovery: What action is required across government to narrow the health gap?', London: The Health Foundation.

Masters, R., Anwar, E., Collins, B., Cookson, R. and Capewell, S. (2017) 'Return on investment of public health interventions: A systematic review', *Journal of Epidemiology and Community Health*, 71: 827–34.

McCartney, M. (2023) 'Semaglutide: Should the media slim down its enthusiasm?', *British Medical Journal*, 380: p624.

McCormack, S., Dunn, D.T., Desai, M., Dolling, D.I., Gafos, M., Gilson, R, et al (2016) 'Pre-exposure prophylaxis to prevent the acquisition of HIV-1 infection (PROUD): Effectiveness results from the pilot phase of a pragmatic open-label randomised trial', *The Lancet*, 387(10013): 53–60. https://doi.org/10.1016/S0140-6736(15)00056-2

McKee, S. (2020) 'The end of Public Health England?', *PharmaTimes*, [online] 17 August, available from: http://www.pharmatimes.com/news/the_end_of_public_health_england_1346934

McNamara, C.L., Green, L., Barlow, P. and Bellis, M.A. (2023) 'The CPTPP trade deal is a major threat to public health and warrants a health impact assessment', *British Medical Journal*, 381: e073302

Metcalfe, S. and Sasse, T. (2023) 'Tackling obesity: Improving policy making on food and health', London: Institute for Government. Available from: https://www.instituteforgovernment.org.uk/sites/default/files/2023-04/tackling-obesity.pdf

Mill, J.S. (1859) 'On Liberty' in J. Gray (ed) *On Liberty and Other Essays* (1991) Oxford: Oxford University Press.

Molina, J.-M., Capitant, C., Spire, B., Pialoux, G., Cotte, L., Charreau, I., et al (2015) 'On-demand preexposure prophylaxis in men at high risk for HIV-1 infection', *New England Journal of Medicine*, 373(23): 2237–46.

Murphie, A. (2023) 'The effect of COVID-19 on the financial sustainability of local government', in A. Bonner (ed) *COVID-19 and Social Determinants of Health*, Bristol: Bristol University Press, pp 170–91.

Murray, R. (2021) 'The Health and Care Bill must require action on health inequalities', *Health Service Journal*, [online] 10 November, available from: https://www.hsj.co.uk/policy-and-regulation/the-health-and-care-bill-must-require-action-on-health-inequalities/7031282.article

National Audit Office. (2014) 'Public Health England's grant to local authorities', HC 888, Session 2014–15, London: National Audit Office. [Online] 16 December, available from: https://www.nao.org.uk/reports/public-health-englands-grant-to-local-authorities/

National Audit Office. (2022) 'Introducing integrated care systems: Joining up local services to improve health outcomes', London: National Audit Office. [Online] 14 October, available from: https://www.nao.org.uk/wp-content/uploads/2022/10/Integrated-Care-Systems-Funding-and-accountability-for-local-health-and-care.pdf

Neville, S. and Borrett, A. (2023) 'UK struggles to get its long-term sick people back into work', *Financial Times*, [online] 16 March, available from: https://www.ft.com/content/74d34caa-e540-4ab8-ab11-be42d152abfc

Neville, S. and Cookson, C. (2023) 'UK lacked resources to scale up fight against Covid-19, inquiry told', *Financial Times*, [online] 22 June, available from https://www.ft.com/content/b203a462-09d9-41dd-891a-e9accf8542c4

NHS England. (2014) 'Five Year Forward View', London: NHS England. [Online] 22 October, available from: https://www.england.nhs.uk/publication/nhs-five-year-forward-view/

NHS England. (2016a) 'Update on commissioning and provision of Pre Exposure Prophylaxis (PREP) for HIV prevention', [online] 21 March, available from: https://www.england.nhs.uk/2016/03/prep/

NHS England (2016b) 'Specialised commissioning annual prioritisation of discretionary investment in service developments 2016/17', Specialised Services Commissioning Committee, 29 November. Accessed through a Freedom of Information request.

NHS England. (2019) 'NHS Long Term Plan', London: NHS England. [Online] 7 January, available from: https://www.longt ermplan.nhs.uk/publication/nhs-long-term-plan/

Nuffield Council on Bioethics. (2007) 'Public health: Ethical issues', [online] November, available from: https://www.nuffieldbioeth ics.org/assets/pdfs/Public-health-ethical-issues.pdf

OECD. (2023) 'Life expectancy at birth (indicator)', OECD iLibrary, [online] https://doi.org/10.1787/27e0fc9d-en

Office for Health Improvement and Disparities (2021), available from: https://www.gov.uk/government/organisations/office-for-health-improvement-and-disparities/about

Office for National Statistics. (2021) 'National life tables – life expectancy in the UK: 2018 to 2020', ONS [online] 23 September, available from: https://www.ons.gov.uk/peoplepop ulationandcommunity/birthsdeathsandmarriages/lifeexpectanc ies/bulletins/nationallifetablesunitedkingdom/2018to2020

Owens, S. (2015) Knowledge, Policy, and Expertise, Oxford: Oxford University Press.

Pettigrew, A., Ferlie, E. and McKee, L. (1992) Shaping Strategic Change: Making Change in Large Organizations. The Case of the National Health Service, London: Sage.

Public Health England. (2015) 'E-cigarettes: An evidence update. A report commissioned by Public Health England', GOV.UK, [online] August, available from: https://assets.publishing.serv ice.gov.uk/government/uploads/system/uploads/attachment_ data/file/733022/Ecigarettes_an_evidence_update_A_report_ commissioned_by_Public_Health_England_FINAL.pdf

Public Health England. (2019) 'Public Health England strategy 2020–25', London: Public Health England. GOV.UK, [online] September, available from: https://assets.publishing.service.gov. uk/government/uploads/system/uploads/attachment_data/file/ 831562/PHE_Strategy_2020-25.pdf

Public Health England. (2020) 'Disparities in the risk and outcomes of COVID-19', London: Public Health England. GOV.UK, [online] August, available from: https://assets.publishing.service. gov.uk/government/uploads/system/uploads/attachment_data/ file/908434/Disparities_in_the_risk_and_outcomes_of_COVID _August_2020_update.pdf

Public Health Wales. (2023) 'Our long-term strategy 2023–2035', [online] March, available from: https://phw.nhs.wales/news/pub lic-health-wales-vision-for-a-healthier-future-for-wales/work ing-together-for-a-healthier-wales/

Ricketts, P. (2021) *Hard Choices: The Making and Unmaking of Global Britain*, London: Atlantic Books.

Rittel, H.W.J. and Webber, M.M. (1973) 'Dilemmas in a general theory of planning', *Policy Sciences*, 4: 155–69. https://doi.org/ 10.1007/BF01405730

Royal College of Physicians. (2016) 'Every breath we take: The lifelong impact of air pollution', RCP London, [online] 23 February, available from: https://www.rcplondon.ac.uk/proje cts/outputs/every-breath-we-take-lifelong-impact-air-pollution

Rutter, H., Savona, N., Glonti, K., Bibby, J., Cummins, S., Finegood, D.T., et al (2017) 'The need for a complex systems model of evidence for public health', *The Lancet*, 390(10112): p2602–4. https://doi.org/10.1016/S0140-6736(17)31267-9

Tedstone, A., Targett, V. and Allen, R. (2015) 'Sugar reduction: The evidence for action', London: Public Health England.

Tehseen, K. Coultas, C. Kieslich, K. and Littlejohns, P. (2023) 'The complexities of integrating evidence-based preventive health into England's NHS: Lessons learnt from the case of PrEP', *Health Research Policy and Systems*, 21(1): 53. doi:10.1186/ s12961-023-00998-4

Vize, R. (2020) 'Controversial from creation to disbanding, via e-cigarettes and alcohol: An obituary of Public Health England', *British Medical Journal*, 2020;371:m4476

Wanless, D. (2002) 'Securing our future health: Taking a long-term view', London: HM Treasury.

Wanless, D. (2004) 'Securing good health for the whole population: Final report', London: The Stationery Office.

Weale, A., Hunter, D.J., Littlejohns, P., Khatun, T. and Johnson, J. (2023) 'Public health by organizational fix?', *Health Economics, Policy and Law*, 18(3): 274–88.

World Health Organization. (2016) 'Health System Transformation: Making it happen', Expert meeting, Madrid, Spain, 17–18 December 2015, Regional Office for Europe, Copenhagen: WHO.

World Health Organization. (2018) 'Leading health system transformation to the next level', Expert meeting, Durham, United Kingdom, 12–13 July 2017, Regional Office for Europe, Copenhagen: WHO.

World Health Organization. (2019) 'Healthy, prosperous lives for all: The European health equity status report', Regional Office for Europe, Copenhagen: WHO.

Index

References to figures appear in *italic* type.